VOICES
FROM FOREVER

RANDALL KELLER

Deciated to
C. Randall Keller
(1915 – 2001)

*To my father, who was always there
for me – even now.*

Voices From Forever
Randall Keller

Copyright © 2009 Randall Keller

All rights reserved, including the right of reproduction
in whole or in part or in any form.

Published in the United States of America.
P.O. Box 44723 / Nottingham, MD 21234-9998
No part of this book may be used or reproduced in any manner
whatsoever without the written permission of the publisher.

Second Printing ISBN: 978-0-615-32881-2

Printed in the United States of America

Contents

Death 1
Voices 27
Seek 49
Magnet 79
Truth 105
Consequences 133
Evidence 161
Hope 187

Death

What do we know about death? The dictionary says it is the end of being alive. That's fairly simple and easy enough to understand, but do we really grasp what that means? And is it accurate? We know what we see – people stop breathing, bodies decay… the person in question "is no more." They're over – ended. But are they really? Do we actually know that?

From the very beginning of mankind's existence there has been talk about some kind of afterlife – people die and they go somewhere else to a different kind of reality. We recognize that the body no longer functions, but there has always been that whole business about what happens to the soul. Christians talk about how the soul is either saved or not saved. In fact, all religions claim something roughly the same though they word it differently. There's talk of joining one's ancestors and loved ones, or of going to see Jesus. Even the pure dust-to-dust crowd seems to acknowledge that there is probably more to it than just dust. Only a true atheist believes there is nothing beyond the moment we die.

But religions and philosophies are sparse on the details, aren't they? And that's true for all of them. They don't have very much specific to say – just a lot of generalities and platitudes, and we usually opt not to press them for those details because it makes sense to us that death is naturally a complete unknown. No one that we know of has ever come back from the dead – not really, and near-death experiences are just as they're labeled – near death, and not accepted as tangible by most people. The one guy we claim to have conquered death, Jesus, went pretty much straight to heaven without filling us in on any of the particulars.

So we accept the widely open-ended concept that when this life is finished, there's probably something else that we don't know very much about except that it will be fabulous. Unless, of course, we were really rotten, and then the afterlife will be horrendous beyond our grasp. Even though I am generalizing this entire issue, I'm not far from being right on the money, because all we can actually say with certainty about death is that it happens.

Scientists have discovered there is energy in the human body, and we know that energy doesn't cease to exist – it changes. That concept might open up a small can of worms for people who really think about it; that this energy could possibly be our soul. But obviously, there's no proof of that, and if I were somehow able to offer you some; even if I served it up on a silver platter in language anyone could understand, you wouldn't believe a word of it. Unless, of course, my evidence corresponded with what you've already been taught. Then you might… maybe. Death is a very precious thing to humans, and we defend our concept of it almost as fervently as we defend our living.

There's death with honor and death with glory. There's untimely death and I've even heard the term "a good death." There's that special death when we claim it's "the best thing." There is a bloody death, a quiet death, a senseless death and a sacrificial death. And you know I could continue – there are a million ways to describe death, and every single one of them is based entirely on speculation and best guesses. We really know absolutely nothing, and there's not one speck of evidence about any of it other than the sorry knowledge that our bodies stop working and decay.

Death may very well be a stepping-stone to a better place, but since we can't prove anything, we just have to be content knowing that death is probably one of those few things in life that we will probably never understand. But death is an incredibly important part of the human condition. The notion that whatever follows life is so nebulous and vague that we'd better make the best of things while we're here, is a huge part of what it means to be human. In a way, we seem to scare ourselves into behaving while we're alive so we don't mess up our place in the afterlife. We better live right, because a sinful life results in spending all eternity in damnation. Think about it. We can't have a lot of really awful people messing up death the same way they messed up life, can we?

But death gets very real when someone close to us passes. There's a whole litany of emotional responses we go through, and sometimes we never really recover from the loss of a loved one. Sometimes, we feel cheated by death and sometimes we wonder what took it so long, but never has it ever been a good thing. Religious views aside, the death of any person is tallied as a loss to someone. Even Adolf Hitler's death was mourned.

Eventually, most of us find ourselves facing a moment when death seems to want us. Maybe we're not even very old; it doesn't make sense – but there it is anyway. Perhaps there's an ambulance and a stretcher; guys in EMT garb are doing things to you and asking you questions. Loved ones are crying or looking worried. There are onlookers. Oh God… strangers watching it all happen. A minute earlier you were fine and life was good. You had plans. And zap – you're confused and a little out of it and you find yourself asking – "is this how it happens for me?"

For me, it was a very hot July night, and I had just left an argument with my ex-wife. I'd put in a long day at work, fought traffic for 90 minutes, spent my last few dollars practically inhaling greasy artery-clogging McDonald's food, and my ex had the audacity to have an issue. I don't remember exactly what it was, but she said something that pushed a button, and there I was driving home cursing and agonizing over every one of the 43 traffic lights en route. The trip was taking forever. It was late. I was pissed, and tired; annoyed and exhausted… and it was so oppressively hot outside.

I must have smoked 4 cigarettes on the way home, and my head was pounding. But to make a very long story short, by the time I arrived home, I felt exceedingly sick. I had trouble breathing. I started sweating, and I couldn't speak very well. I commented about my jaw hurting, and my neck was tight and quite painful. Finally, I just could not go on. I remember my lady friend saying, "Are you okay? Are you having a heart attack or something?"

"Yes." And I didn't even think twice about that answer. As soon as I heard the words, I knew that was right. She dialed 911. I heard her tell them the information – calmly, methodically... but I could see the fear on her face. My body was in revolt, and I was trying to ignore an intense pain in my chest that seemed to keep getting worse.

It only took a couple of minutes before the ambulance arrived. I wasn't sure what was going on by that time, but soon enough I was on the stretcher wondering where all those people came from, and wondering whether I was going to die or not.

Now, I know this story is hardly unique. I know it's actually pretty typical, but the point is that I had no idea what was going to happen, and dying seemed like a distinct possibility. A few minutes earlier, death was the last thing on my mind, but for some inexplicable reason, I was in an ambulance listening to some guy on a radio tell the hospital about my vital signs.

I honestly thought I was going to die. My mind kept

racing through all sorts of horrific scenarios, so I decided that since life was possibly going to be over, I should spend those remaining moments praying and repenting. I felt slightly blessed because I had arrived at the end of my life with some extra time to set things right with God. And I was sorry for everything – I wanted to cover all the bases; I accepted culpability for things I didn't even know I did. Of course, the elephant in the room is that I didn't die.

Which brings me to my father. He did die, and I wasn't prepared for that either, even though I knew full well he was on the doorstep. And when he did pass (eight weeks after my own little dance with the reaper), I didn't properly mourn. I got the 3:00 a.m. call from my mother at the hospice that he was gone, and that she needed me to come. She was there at the end, and he spoke a few private words and then faded gently away. By the time I got there, forty minutes later, he was like a stone monument of himself – cold and hard and completely lifeless.

It wasn't anything like sleeping without breathing – it was totally clear that life had ended. He was no longer there. And weirdly enough, I looked for him in the dark corner of the ceiling; sitting in the chair by the door; hovering at the foot of the bed. I looked everywhere, because he surely wasn't in that body, and I knew... I just knew he had to be somewhere else. Without thinking about it, I knew his soul had vacated and relocated. It was just a feeling, and I wouldn't dare suggest there was any precognition, but I felt like he was still there – somewhere. So, I looked around the room knowing full well I wouldn't see him anywhere.

I would like to have attempted some sort of goodbye; maybe kissed his forehead; something. I definitely wanted to tell him I loved him and that he was a great father. I wanted to let him know that he would always be in my memory, and that I would try to become as good a man as he was.

And you can imagine that I would want to wax poetic about this. We've all lost someone, and we all know the kind of stuff that comes racing to the front of our minds and mocks us. Some kind of sadistic reminder of our own failure to do right by our deceased loved one – deserved or not – takes over all other thought and burns a hole right in the middle of our hearts.

So, I never really mourned my father's death. I don't know if that was because I had just experienced my own encounter with death, or because I had expected it to happen. But I never shed a tear; refrained from commenting on his life… I was pretty quiet about it all, and reserved. So much so that I wondered if there was something wrong with me to be so callous. I didn't have any issues with the man – there were no pent-up emotions about a bad childhood; no resentments or anything negative whatsoever. He had dementia and sometimes I had to be forceful just to control him. I regretted doing that; felt kind of guilty at times, but it had to be done; and if my finesse was lacking, well, I did the best I could. Still, throughout the usual funeral parlor/graveyard thing, I was acting as though it was just another day at the office; just another inconvenience, and I was duty-bound to graciously endure.

When they lowered the casket and the people started to move away and head back into their lives, I wondered if mine would ever be the same again. I wondered if I could make it on my own without him in my life. I told myself the usual things – he would be there in my heart; he would be there whenever I needed his guidance – in spirit. I pretty much thoroughly convinced myself that all would be well, lives would continue, and that it was all a part of life. Dying was part of living.

And indeed, it is. So, as I sped through my life in the years that followed, I thought of my father a lot. And I came to grips rather easily with the notion that I was just not the kind of person who mourned normally. I was somehow stronger than most and better equipped to handle life's distress. I told myself I could be the rock in everyone's life; that he had passed that mantle to me, and whenever I needed his advice, I would find it by remembering how he lived and guided me.

But five years later, while recuperating from my third heart attack, I found myself standing at the back door in my kitchen, smoking a cigarette and weeping like a baby. I was praying at first – I wanted God to take care of my dad, and better late than never, I was really quite overcome with grief. I simply wished he was still here, and when the praying was finished, I started talking directly to him; told him how I truly felt about him. I apologized for things I did to wrong him, and praised him for the kind of person he was. I cried through the whole thing – maybe for three hours or so – until I didn't have any more tears to shed. And when it was all over, I had mourned. I had finally grieved the passing of perhaps the most influential person in my life. I felt like that proverbial weight had been lifted – as if my life could only be better for having done it.

Fascinating, I thought. Such a simple thing. You go nuts for a few hours, cry out some tears, deal with some emotions, and voila – mourning a fait accompli. But, I've since decided that it doesn't work like that. I think mourning never stops. Feeling awful might end, but not mourning. Mourning gets too deep into who you are for anyone to ever really let go of it for good. It helps to mold you from then on; it teaches you things you could never have known otherwise. It dissipates, but it lingers. Mourning makes you appreciate its opposite, and it builds you up and prepares you for the next time you have to go through it all again. Maybe you will lose a wife or a husband. Or worse, a child. You need what you learn from mourning – a lot.

Maybe death isn't actually about the deceased at all, but about the living, because at some point, you finally understand that death is as much a part of life as breathing. Its inevitable. It is probably the singular feature in life that's guaranteed, and is actually the only thing we all have in common. We all have to go through it. We all lose people we love and we all teeter dangerously on the edge of our mortality.

Nobody wants to die, but once you do it, you're either on

your way to another existence, or you're dust. There's only one thing to learn from death if you're the deceased, and whatever that lesson is will be quite obvious before anyone has even called the undertaker. But the people who are left behind have all sorts of things to go through, not the least of which are a number of items to learn about themselves as a result of your untimely fatality.

For the living, death's timing is never very good, and no matter how much you've come to expect it, it always comes with about as much warning as a heart attack.

I remember very clearly lying on the operating table just this year, and listening to what was going on around me. I remember realizing that something really bad had just happened, and it took a few seconds to sink in just what that was. I started to fade away – everything just got farther away and a little strange. Right before I stopped living, I remember thinking just one word – "Now?"

I didn't have very much time to get too shaken, but it was all so incredulous, and I felt completely out of control. I couldn't fight it, there was no pain… I was losing consciousness incredibly fast, and at the last split second, I understood. But now? Really? Like this? Fascinating. And then… there was nothing. Not just darkness and quiet. Nothing peaceful or even unmerciful. No bright lights. No other world or alternative universe creeping into my consciousness. Just nothing. A nothing so empty of anything that when they brought me back, I remember saying out loud "That was weird. I think." I didn't know.

It certainly didn't feel like there was any sort of afterlife available when it happened, but then I could tell I had been brought back – something in my mind instantly knew that had happened. But between the fading away and the bringing back, there wasn't anything.

Now maybe I was only gone for a few seconds, and maybe it takes time for the good stuff to start happening. Maybe God wasn't ready to take me, so there wasn't any need to see the brochures or view the orientation video. Maybe a few seconds longer and I would have seen the famous bright light and recognized deceased friends and family trying to help me move on. Maybe under normal circumstances there would have been angels there to escort me wherever it is souls go.

But even though it wasn't a terrible experience, I can assure anyone reading this that I can't imagine wanting to go through it again. It may not have been traumatic, but it sure as hell wasn't fun. And I'm not certain, but I don't think I've gotten over it yet. Such a brief moment in the middle of what has become a long life – just a few completely uneventful seconds, and yet the impact is so surprisingly all encompassing.

And I told everyone I met over the next few weeks, and I still do if I get the chance, that nothing in life prepared me for it. I will always remember that for a very small amount of time I was dead enough to not want to be dead ever again. And even though there's nothing I can do about the inevitability of finally one day passing on, even though the afterlife is supposed to be so satisfying, death will always be my very last choice. And that's the duty of being human, after all – to stay alive; to do whatever it takes to survive.

But you know, this is not meant to comprise a comprehensive tome on death. What this is really all about is the paranormal implications of death. Because unless you've missed the metaphysical allusion to all of this, there's very probably something going on when the party's over, and whatever it is might just possibly be noticeable. It's not inconceivable that our technology and understanding of our own world can finally give us some insight into the next world. Or perhaps more than just insight.

Who's to say there's no such thing as parallel universes; alternate physical worlds in the same time and space. If energy doesn't die, what happens to it? What is it about particle theory and quantum mechanics that seem like handbooks to the beyond? Could there be ten dimensions? Twelve? More?

So, when the question "what made you get into all this paranormal stuff?" is posed, my answer is, of course – ta dah – death. The death of my father made me do it. I was content being unconcerned and uninspired until he went and passed away on me and led me down this road to perdition – the paranormal highway – full of devils and ghosts and scary noises and creepy Halloween-like stuff.

You can safely assume that curiosity is the culprit, but let's be honest here… how many of us wouldn't want to know something about the afterlife if we could? Not very many. And if the afterlife is just full of ghosts, weird goings-on and disembodied voices… how bloody cool is that, right? I mean, a lot of people say "I don't believe in that rubbish" but if we're all very honest with ourselves, deep down inside we're not really sure what we think about the paranormal, are we? But one thing is very clear – what we have labeled the paranormal is undeniably linked with death.

As a young teen, on one of those nights when my friend Michael and I were supposedly sleeping at one another's house, we found ourselves instead walking the streets at five in the morning. We were fortunate enough to be in front of another friend's house when she returned from the late shift at her summer waitress job. She told us all about a blue lady who floated in her back yard every morning at just about that very time.

Now the blue lady was the spirit of an unhappy young woman who was buried in the family plot of the Perry Hall Mansion, and that family plot just so happened to be in our friend's back yard. Well, our lady friend spun such a great story that we vowed to come back the next night to catch this blue lady once and for all.

And we returned with three other guys and sat in an old 1961 Pontiac Gran Prix waiting for the blue lady to rise and float over our friend's yard once again. We had cameras and binoculars – maybe a beer or two, and we were ready. Five wannabe adults doing a very adult thing – lying to our parents about where we were, and trying to be quiet so as not to encourage the neighbors to call the cops before our ghoulish endeavor could be completed.

Five o'clock took forever to get there, and at first, there was nothing. No blue lady – not even a pale mist. Not even fog. But then… then she started to emerge. First the driver of the car saw her – proclaiming in a hushed whisper, pointing toward the high grass in our friend's backyard – "I see her," he said. And one by one, everyone in the car saw her. Everyone but me.

"She's right there near the corner of the house, Keller. Can't you see that? Are you blind? Keller can't see her!" They were amazed. I kept looking, but I just didn't see a thing. I even volunteered to get out of the car and walk over there, but that was verboten. What if she got me? They couldn't do anything to help me. If we all stuck together… Such talk. I remember thinking that if I saw a blue lady rise from the earth and float around a suburban barbecue pit, I'd be too petrified to converse about it. I just kept thinking "they're not scared enough." I would be terrified – a lot. And really, who wouldn't be?

I always believed they saw nothing at all that night, but I suppose it was fun to pretend. It was definitely something to do on a warm summer night, and I'm sure our friend the waitress had some laughs watching us from her air conditioned bedroom. It was, in fact, a hoax and the funny thing is, these guys still maintain they saw the blue lady, even though the waitress admitted she made it all up.

Was I the only one able to hold on to reality that night? Maybe I was just one of those people who knows what he sees. But I do wish I had seen her – even now. That night ushered in years and years – decades – of non-belief. Ghosts weren't real and no one was going to convince me they were. And even when I'd finally retreated from that position just enough to entertain the possibility, I always knew it would require proof.

My sister was too quick to hear footsteps on the third floor at my grandmother's home. A friend was certain he'd seen his dead aunt when he was dressing one morning. Another saw his grandfather, who offered girlfriend advice. There was a lady who died in the house I'd just sank my life savings into, and my middle child's nightmares were of an old woman she did not know.

None of these things were believable to me. It was all humbug. It was all folklore and great fun, but it wasn't real. God didn't operate that way. It wasn't a supernatural world – there were rules of physics and gravity for God's sake. And people's souls went to heaven. I'd never seen, heard, smelled or tasted a ghost, and I never would. The dead stay dead. End of discussion.

Until my father died. That sweet old man somehow managed to turn me upside down and shake the sense right out of my skeptical brain. He was gone, and I had grieved, and I missed him. I read a book that suggested some pretty interesting possibilities – Allison DuBois' *We Are Their Heaven*. And she spoke about deceased loved ones as hanging around and coming to visit and spending time. Not because they were chained to earth in some kind of purgatorial agony, but because they wanted to be there – right by our side just… chillin'. Imagine that! An outrageous concept to say the least, but… well, shucks… I might be able to believe in that.

I believed her enough to think about it. I mean, what a great way to have heaven, right? A kind of resort-like place where people come and go, but much hipper. How are the kids doing, Ma? "Let's go see!" And off they go – checking out the kids. Hanging around… I dunno… in closets, or under beds, or wherever a ghost might go. Up high, maybe… right there in the corner of my room. Say… on my birthday, for instance. My grandparents, deceased aunts and uncles, older cousins, friends of the family, and my dad – all of them crammed into my little room just checking me out, singing happy birthday in ghostspeak, and who knows what else!

And I make light of it, because ghost-stuff is serious business, so ya gotta find the humor when you can. But I began to totally buy into all of it. I loved the idea of deceased loved ones coming to hang out. It was comforting. What a great life for them. My dad could go anywhere, do anything, see anyone he wanted to – forever. I just loved it!

And this hanging out concept made sense to me. Everything about life is systematic, and this idea really smelled like a system. Everything in the universe revolves around a very complex series of predictable events. There are scientific reasons that the earth rotates the way it does. There are rules of mathematics that can't be challenged, and the laws of physics are orderly and prescribed. Why would death and the afterlife be any different? Every piece of what we know is part of one incredibly complex system. There are actions and reactions at every level of being, and the results are easily foreseeable; in fact, unavoidable.

Everything has a purpose in this universe, and while we are full of questions and might not know very many of the answers, everything is like a part of a jigsaw puzzle, and all the pieces somehow miraculously fit. And that much, we do know, so I think its more probable than not that the things we don't know very much about have to be ordered as well. It defies any kind of logic to invoke the notion that even a single element of reality would be random. It may appear to be so, but as we learn about things that have been previously unknown, we find time and time again that its all a very complex and beautiful regularity – part of a system.

Having a system preside over our existence doesn't allow for most of the ghost stories we all love. Why would God, or whatever creator you want to believe in, allow such arbitrary nonsense? Spirits that are tethered to a piece of furniture or a house don't fit into a scientific system, or it would be like that for every spirit and every house. The universe only punishes obsolescence and it never ever judges. This system doesn't care about anything except itself. And if you like, if you want to suggest that God is, in actuality, the creator and landlord of this system, what makes us even entertain the notion that He would allow such haphazard silliness.

But! And there is always a "but," isn't there? We know

for a fact that energy does not end – it changes, and yet the energy within our bodies disappears when we die. Where does it go? Another plane of life maybe? Perhaps it is now governed by an entirely new set of physical laws. Perhaps it goes nowhere, and simply cannot be detected by our unfortunate limitations. Maybe our souls – our energy – only mutate; become like infrared or ultraviolet, imperceptible to those few parts of the system we actually understand. Perhaps it moves to a subsystem, with its own set of logic and governance. What if up was down, or if the only way to communicate was telepathically? What if everything was so uniquely different from what we know as reality, that it exists completely independent of our ability to see, hear, or smell it?

It's not so inconceivable to think that death is as consistent and as organized as everything else in the universe. All things have properties and a place, and all things operate within a set of possibilities. And as people, we cannot exist in other dimensions, and in turn, our souls are only partially able to exist in ours.

Kinda complex, I know, but to me it is more wise to think of death as just another part of the system. A part we will probably never fully comprehend, because we are not capable; we're not constructed to handle it. Until we ourselves die, that is.

Thinking of death as a whole other place is a lot like the traditional concept of heaven and hell. But we insist on thinking about these places in terms we understand, knowing full well it can't possibly be that way. We couldn't be right, right? But whether it is heaven, or seven planes of something else; whether it's mental or energy only; even if it's in another galaxy, or sharing the same exact space as we currently occupy, the dead are transformed and live in an altered state.

And if you think this is in conflict with God or scripture, think again. There are no verses that explain any part of the system. That knowledge is like the apple on the tree of life in Eden all those millennia ago – we can look and we can touch, but we cannot partake. And maybe this is not because God wants to keep his secrets to himself, but because none of that knowledge is of any real use to us.

This comforts me because it means all my fantastic deceased relatives are still around somewhere, and as the medium says, they're hanging out. In death, their reality is different from ours – their possibilities more endless. Indeed, the afterlife has never been labeled as restrictive – certainly not as life is on earth. So I love the hanging around concept. A lot.

In fact, I loved it so much, and I was so convinced my dad was there visiting from time to time, that I decided I needed to communicate with him. And I bought a digital voice recorder. I was going to make EVP. I'd seen it on TAPS and other places. I could do that, and maybe he'd speak. Maybe there'd be that faint voice everyone else got, passing out life wisdom aimed at me, or just saying hello… It was worth a shot. Why not?

Well, if you don't know what an EVP is, the letters stand for Electronic Voice Phenomenon. In other words, you turn on a recording device and when you listen back, there are possibly disembodied voices evident on the recording. Oh I know, it sounds too strange for words, but fortunately, these days most people understand the concept.

Well, when you first hear your very own EVP... one that came from your recorder and was discovered by you... one that says an actual word or words that make sense... there is no other way to put it than to say that your life changes, and nothing is ever the same ever again.

My first EVP called me by name. It said, "Randy, ya gotta change." Nothing about Satan or "get out!" No cries for help from a tortured soul. There was a very matter of fact, female voice that called my name and passed out that actual advice. And you know what that did to me, don't you? I mean, I don't have to tell you, do I? Yes, of course I was gonna do it again! Probably a lot. And sure, I went to great lengths to make certain the voice didn't belong to someone living. But besides all of that, it was like 10,000 volts of unseen electric everything, and it hit me full square in the... well, everywhere.

And I still love my wife and children. I still try to be polite and hold the door for little old ladies. I love spaghetti just as much as I always did. I still don't preach from street corners about the Second Coming, and I like football, serious brunettes, and just holding a really good Nikon. I am still who I always was, but I'm different, because now I understand something. Now, I know.

And you can say what you will about my sanity or my salvation – doesn't bother me a bit. Certain things will never be the same again for me, because the other side spoke up. And it called me by name, and gave me advice. And since that day, I've recorded several thousand EVP – some just as profound as that first one; others not so much; still others are silly and obscure. But someone is speaking, and by God, I'm listening.

So I guess I'm redefining the word death from now on. The dictionary may say that death is the end of being alive but that can't be right, can it? Maybe it's the word "alive" that needs some redefinition. Maybe our definitions of both words are not broad enough. Or maybe what we refer to as life is only a part of what constitutes actual existence. It is possible that existence never really ends at all – just becomes something else. Like the energy in our bodies, it changes.

And while I can't come up with a suitable explanation of what I really think death is really all about, I'm no longer willing to see it as an end. A frightening, incredibly unknown reconstitution of who and what we are – maybe, but an ending – no. And granted, a lot of this is pure semantics, but I think it's something we will be forced to accept differently from now on.

Modern technology has equipped us with the means to measure and record things we will never ever be able to experience with any of our senses. This wide array of hidden wonders has opened our eyes wide enough to challenge the very foundation of our understanding of life, so why not death?

But wait. Let me make something clear. I'm a Christian, and I like being one. All the things that some people make fun of Christians for believing are the very same things I like the most. I like the idea that I can be saved. Salvation can't be anything but a good thing. Having someone who is all-knowing and all-powerful in charge of "the system" is pretty reassuring.

Being a Christian can be functionally complex at times, but it's also the simplest thing in the world – you either believe Christ died for your sins, or you don't. And everything else about the religion is up for negotiation. There are so many denominations that you have to wonder if we're all reading the same Bible, but it all distills down to salvation – afterlife. All these diversities of expression – these different Christian churches – are all on the same page when it comes to that core issue. So if you want to speak in tongues or take a vow of silence – feel free. Even if you're wrong, Jesus died for your sins, so its all good.

Yes, I know there's more to it than that. I know I'm oversimplifying. Its not up to me to try to cover all the beliefs and practices of all the many sects and groups that call themselves Christian. Even if I wanted to, it would take a lifetime to categorize them and deal with them all adequately. But that core belief of faith in Jesus speaks directly to what I've been talking about – death. The single most important part about being a Christian deals with the afterlife. And whether or not I eat meat on Friday or believe in abortion, its that afterlife I am most concerned with – surviving death.

And I certainly have no interest in proselytizing, and I don't state my own religious beliefs as a means to diminish anyone else's. I fully understand that there are billions of people who don't believe in Jesus. But I do, and everything I say about life and death is filtered through the eyes of a Christian. Everything I feel about the subject of death comes from my faith, and I cannot ignore that.

The Bible refers to death as being without God – the opposite of salvation, which is found in the presence of God. It doesn't talk about an end at all. Our lives go on after death if we are to believe scripture. We leave these bodies in the dust and our souls transform. I always read the scripture to mean that death was simply another state – like a rite of passage or something. Scripture doesn't mention anything about the nothingness I experienced on the operating table, or the white light so many others have seen. There are no details because death is a whole other existence that we cannot possibly understand.

Our lives, as we know them in this reality, are comparable to larvae, if you will. We are the beginning of a cycle. We find ourselves in the lowest state here on earth, and death is a requirement before we can move on. Our dying is every bit as important as our birth. And this system of movement – from one state to another is largely undefined.

But we have filled in the blanks. Humans think of

death with a great deal of suspicion, so we invent our own personal insight about what awaits us on the other side. Most of us have a much clearer notion of what hell is like as opposed to a rather incomplete understanding of what heaven will offer. And this is because we fear hell so much. We are convinced that heaven is wonderful, and scripture tells us it is so extraordinary that our minds cannot even begin to grasp how desirable it is. So, we don't worry about heaven – that's good enough for us. We only worry about getting there.

And that worry is the problem. We spend so much time focusing on the good deeds and the evil among us that we lose sight of the simple truth that death is just the next step through the reality of life – eternal life, because energy doesn't cease, it changes.

Death is not the destruction or extinction of us. It is, instead, a door on our way through one part of "the system." And when we get to wherever it is our death is taking us, I have no doubt there will be other doors to traverse in our future.

Now, of course, all I have said in defense of death is my opinion, and since mankind has yet to offer a single artifact from the beyond, that opinion is as good as anyone's. But consider this… Now that there are voices to be heard from somewhere other than here; voices from entities whose existence does not equate with the logic of our own; voices that know us and speak to us knowingly… At this time and with that small splash of knowledge, what other conclusion can we draw than to say that death is not the end of being alive at all, but the beginning of the next step that we all must take.

Voices

I went into the whole EVP thing without expectations. I didn't know whether I really wanted to hear anything or not. I thought I did, and the very first time I decided to try was at 2:00 a.m. – sitting alone in the living room with my brand new Sony digital recorder in my hand. Unfortunately, I couldn't bring myself to even make the attempt. I'd bought the recorder two months earlier and kept forgetting to try. Maybe I was putting it off. So, looking back, I may have been apprehensive about the results I might get. I knew that if I did get voices, things would be different from then on, and I don't think I knew what to do or what to even think.

During those two months, my doorbell started ringing at all times of the day – by itself. There was never anyone there when I went to the door. My front door includes a commanding view of the area, and I would have seen someone pranking or whatever, so I was positive the doorbell was ringing without human initiation. And it very well could have been a short in the circuit or been triggered by a car alarm switch in the neighborhood. Knowing my neighborhood, that was unlikely, so I began to assume that this was, instead, the result of a spirit who decided it wanted my attention. That's an unwise and probably wrong assumption to make, but I thought perhaps if a spirit wanted to announce his or her presence or make some kind of contact, this would be a good way to do it. Ringing the doorbell at strange hours is bound to get one's attention, and I took it as an invitation to converse.

But that first EVP session ended without so much as pressing the on button. I obtusely searched for the right words to begin, and the longer I waffled, the dumber I felt. I didn't want to merely be talking to myself, but I was probably more concerned with the idea of potentially opening a door to the unknown and inviting unwanted evil spirits into my life. So I froze on that first night - long enough to convince myself to go to bed.

Not long after, my sister was coming to town from Chicago. That was a rare occurrence. She hadn't been been able to visit toward the end of my father's life, and there had been no contact with him during his last months. That upset my mother, and the two of us spent more than a few conversations as to why my sister stayed away when he was clearly on his way out.

So, when little sis announced her first visit since the funeral, I decided to attempt an EVP session at my mother's house while she was visiting. I thought there would be an emotional charge to things, and if my dad actually was "hanging around" he would definitely be there to see her. As a result, I planned to ask a bunch of specific questions and attempt to be professional about it, but when the time came to actually engage in the EVP session, I couldn't bring myself to do it. Instead, I planted the recorder on a counter, and pressed "record."

For the next twenty minutes, we all sat around the kitchen table and talked a blue streak – there were six of us. This made for a lot of people in one kitchen, and you can imagine how chaotic the recording was. After twenty minutes, we all left for a restaurant, and I continued to record while we were gone.

Two hours later, you can hear us unlocking the door, followed by the swell of conversation as we slowly came inside. There was another twenty minutes of chaos, and then I remembered the recorder and shut it off, promising my sister to go over the recordings before she left for home.

Now, I am certain that anyone would come to the same conclusion I did – those minutes of chaos would be useless for EVP, but the two hours of quiet time in the house might just be productive. That's exactly how I looked at it, and the next day, I began to listen. I heard all sorts of noises – bangs, clicks, the sound of rustling paper. I heard cars drive by and children across the street. I heard the air conditioner turn on and off, and something that sounded like glasses being clinked. I was enthralled, not to mention elated, that I had captured the sounds of spirits at play in my mother's house. In fact, I pictured my father walking through the house doing all sorts of things, and being responsible for all those noises.

Well, I won't bore you with the investigation surrounding those sounds, except to tell you that over the course of the next two weeks, I was able to locate and account for all but two of them. Each one was a natural occurrence – house noises, and they were all easily explainable. There was nothing I'd recorded that was paranormal.

Well… there was a very soft whistle – two notes, very faint, and it sounded a little different from the other non-mechanical sounds. But it made me wonder what I might hear if I listened very carefully to the chaos recorded while everyone was in the kitchen.

It was in that chaos that I managed to isolate two relatively clear EVP – my first voices, and they clearly did not belong to anyone who was in the house. You could hear people come and go from the room, and I started to make note of where everyone was. I was the only male present, so when I recorded a male voice calling my niece a "pretty young thing" – words I did not say – I realized that there was something going on. And it was both creepy and astonishing. Everyone who was there that night gathered around at one point or another and listened to those two EVP and each one of them knew those voices did not belong to us.

In the coming months, I initiated many EVP sessions at my mother's home, and quite a few at my own home, in response to my ringing doorbell. I recorded voices every single time. It didn't matter what the circumstances were, there was some kind of EVP present on the recording. I went to great lengths to determine if these EVP voices belonged to one of us in the room, or if it could be some kind of electronic interference. Only after assuring myself that all possible explanations were exhausted was I willing to label the sound clip in question as an EVP.

Throughout the rest of that first summer, and well into the fall, the number of EVP I recorded dramatically increased, and I identified as many as 14 different voices at my mother's house. Most of the time, the recordings there were with only the two of us present, while we sat at the kitchen table and talked about whatever came to mind. Throughout the recordings, the 14 voices commented on what we were saying or doing, talked to one another, and occasionally took the time to pontificate about the error of our ways. They called us by name, mentioned other family members, and cursed at us from time to time.

I assigned personalities to the voices. I decided that each one was obviously a deceased relative who had come to hang out and join the festivities. I labeled the whispering man as my father, and the rather loud female voice belonged to my Aunt Dorothy. But other than those two, nothing said by the EVP voices was definitive enough to make ownership of the words assignable. I continued to make assumptions simply because I wanted to attach a face to each voice. I didn't even give it a second thought, at first, but somewhere down the line I realized a truth.

There was no way to prove who belonged to any of those

voices. Oh sure, some of them seemed like they could be my father, and only my aunt would say such things. There were names thrown about within the EVP themselves – Uncle Nick was referred to as Albert (his never-used real name), and mention was also made of my parent's marriage. Still, it began to dawn on me that it was probably just as possible that any spirit would know personal things about me, and could fool me into making false conjectures. Maybe these spirits could read my mind. Maybe they all knew one another. Maybe all those voices weren't human at all. Maybe maybe maybe…

From that point on, I assumed the practice of not attaching faces to the voices. I realized that even when I asked for a name, if I actually got one, that it could be a lie. In fact, while this was going on at my mother's on such a grand scale, I was receiving some smaller results at my own home with different voices. And the ones at home had already done just what I suspected – lied to me.

I realize the temptation to assign ownership of a particular voice to someone we love who has passed away is a temptation almost too great to pass up. I know better than most that these voices are seductive – they make you hear much more than they actually say. And it's fun! It's great to imagine one's family hovering somewhere in the room, making comments on your life or giving advice; watching over you and possibly protecting you.

However, while EVP are many things, they are not frivolous. They can be funny and silly sometimes, and they make the occasional profound statement. They offer us only infinitesimal insight into the next world, they comment on the state of humanity, and they even criticize politicians. They seem to be aware of every aspect of our lives – from our illnesses to our love affairs. And they sometimes even ask for help and exhibit great angst for their own situation – whatever that really may be. But they are not the stuff of playtime. Once you have ruled out all the real world explanations concerning the origin of an EVP; once all the possible analysis has completely disqualified some kind of fakery, what you are left with is, quite frankly, a disembodied voice. A voice that comes from somewhere outside the human experience. Call it heaven or hell, purgatory, or the space between the cracks of time – these voices are otherworldly, and they should not be taken lightly.

EVP are not parlor tricks or games. They are not meant to be entertainment, although they are always entertaining. They are not good times on a Friday night, or a hip replacement for the Ouija Board. So, I will emphasize this again: EVP are disembodied voices! They are paranormal, and that means, by definition, they are unable to be explained or understood in terms of scientific knowledge. Oh sure, we hear them and we record them. But we don't know anything more than the fact that they exist.

Everyone who has ever been involved in this kind of endeavor probably has their own explanation. I have heard that EVP are aliens, recordings locked in granite that have escaped, demons, angels, people in limbo from God knows where… And of course, they are also the spirits of deceased people. But… prove it to me. Tell me something that will convince me that the EVP I personally recorded belong to anyone in particular, or fit into any of the above categories. Tell me they come from an alien named Bob, and I'll argue just as effectively that they are anything and everything else.

But I am left with a quandary, because I trust that bona fide EVP are the voices of the deceased. I really believe that. I also believe they are quite possibly angels or demons. I believe this because there seems to be some strand of logic in the phenomenon and you already know that I believe in the logic of the universe – seen or unseen. The quandary comes when I realize that what I believe is of little consequence. As surely as I hear a disembodied voice on my recorder, there is no proof as to its origin or ownership – only that it exists.

Still, there are definitely voices. Of that, there is no doubt. For anyone who has tried to hear the voices and succeeded, their presence is undeniable – skeptics be damned. There are skeptics who just will not accept the EVP voice as true. These people will never be convinced, and will go to great lengths to make their case – even if it results in slowing any progress made in the paranormal field. These people are like the Inquisition in both their attitude and their lack of true interest in what's worth knowing about the world. This, of course, makes the paranormal investigator a latter day Galileo – searching for truth and knowledge within a field of study that currently incorporates less science than it does mumbo jumbo. Like the emerging science of Galileo's day, the paranormal is expected to do no more than support presently misinformed thinking. As a result, the paranormal investigator of today is generally classified as a weirdo and a freak.

Paranormal investigators are usually accused of doing bad science without scientific method. After all, should we be expected to accept the word of a housewife in Hoboken who has convincing video of a full bodied apparition? How about the guy who has done exhaustive work with a full spectrum camera and has photographed unexplainable shadows not visible to the human eye? Surely this is not going to be considered evidence, right?

Well, of course, I am being ridiculous to make a point: paranormal research seems doomed to struggle under a cloud of suspicion unequaled in any field of science today. And the fact that it is progressed by housewives, and computer geeks, off-duty security guards, electronics wizards, camera enthusiasts – indeed, people from all walks of life – only adds credence to the skeptic's claims that the field is not science at all, but a bunch of hooey, full of hobgoblins and parlor tricks from non-scientists and overly imaginative social misfits.

Does anyone want to fund a paranormal study or an experiment? My guess is no. And for those paranormal endeavors that have received funding, I would bet the dollar amounts are diminutive to say the least when compared to the amount of money given to learn what dolphins really think. This is partly the case because it is a relatively new field of study, but in my opinion, it is largely due to the skeptic within our society who has demonized all notion of learning beyond what we already know for certain.

Someone in the 1950s is reported to have said that it was no longer required to fund any more scientific research because mankind has already discovered everything there was to discover. Needless to say, no one paid any attention to him, but I see the modern-day skeptic in this line of thinking. Just the same, precautions need to be taken in paranormal research, and since EVP qualify as paranormal research, it is absolutely necessary that I do everything I can to find an explanation before I label a voice as an EVP – as paranormal. And I do just that, but it doesn't really matter – the modern-day, so-called skeptic is never satisfied.

I know the difference between a television broadcast and an EVP. And I know all about radio waves being received by digital recorders. I understand that there are all sorts of really weird things that can cause so-called voices to seem as if they are coming from the great beyond. But, show me a skeptic who insists there's always interference from a cell phone, or a television, or a ham radio broadcast, and I will show you a guy who will absolutely never believe in EVP. And listening to such an individual, much less taking what he says to heart, is a waste of time for anyone interested in the paranormal.

Perhaps that sounds a bit harsh, and the paranormal community would probably disagree with my attitude, but the truth for me is that the devices in question do not broadcast in whispers while knowing my name or commenting on my habits. No radio broadcast is going to call me Randy, tell me that smoking is bad while I am in the actual process of lighting up, and then return 30 seconds later to mention my sister Margo by name. When I speak into a recorder and ask whoever is present to speak up, cell phone interference is not going to say that "talking makes me hurt" in a robotic high pitched and pained female voice.

Of course, I know this is not the common wisdom or the acceptable attitude to take. I am supposed to be open for debunking. And I am, but the skeptic living inside of me is equally unconvinced of these strangely concocted excuses. I will accept the idea that it doesn't seem logical for a disembodied voice to exist at all, but not that every EVP is a weird combination of syllables from police scanners that coincidentally happen to fit the question being asked at the moment. And asking me, or anyone, to believe that the thousands of EVP that have been recorded are all coincidental receptions from various and sundry interfering media is asking a bit too much.

It's one thing to suggest that I made it all up; that I faked the voices for some kind of cheap thrill – some kind of stupid hoax on an unsuspecting and gullible world. That's one thing. But to try and arbitrarily dismiss the paranormal pedigree of every single captured EVP is more dense than the concept itself could ever be. It's just a stubborn attitude that seems clearly bent on learning nothing.

Hearing an EVP is a memorable experience. Hearing hundreds of them is a revelation. And this is not something you are likely to forget – ever – but to dismiss them glibly as a plethora of coincidences is some form of mental illness, I think. What are the odds of so many coincidental voice recordings being made? Anyone know? I'm not gonna waste one second finding the answer to that, because its astronomical.

And yet, there seem to be quite a few people intent on writing off every single EVP with one or more of a series of convenient and trivializing explanations. I call it the weather balloon defense. And I'm told that as a paranormal investigator (which I do not actually claim to me) I am duty-bound to dismiss anything as evidence unless I can prove it isn't one of these coincidental happenings – guilty before innocent. With this kind of scrutiny, mankind would not have cured a single disease; there would be no scientific advances suitable for the inquisitional world we would be enduring. Hell, we might not even have ice cream! We would still be in the dark ages running away from the sheriff and his band of thugs on horseback in chain mail.

Does that mean I am suggesting that every EVP ever recorded is a guaranteed slam-dunk of paranormal evidence? Of course not. But don't insult me and try to tell me that I'm too stupid to differentiate between an interactive disembodied voice and the most recent broadcast of Mister Ed on a local channel. I know when someone is talking to me. I can tell the difference between an intelligent conversation and electronic bleedthrough.

And I'm not even talking about those heavily enhanced, metallic sounding EVP that barely pass for speech. I don't consider them EVP either. They're like sound effects, or bad reception on a two-way radio. No, I'm talking about voices that sound like they're in the room with you; that sound like you're not alone – voices you do not hear when they happen. I'm talking about voices that know the unique name of your deceased Aunt BeeBee Lux, or her brother-in-law, Ed Robinson. I'm talking about voices that repeat your name over and over – with a different inflection each time.

Sound like I'm a little peeved or something - like maybe my chaps were rubbing just a little too much on my thighs? Well, I am sometimes upset. Skepticism is fine with me. I like it in fact. I think we should be very much the skeptic when we enter into this sort of enterprise, but there comes a time when you have to abandon the doubt and embrace the possible. It's very much like wanting your favorite team to win the big game and then denying the final score when they lose. Eventually, you have to accept that the team has lost and eventually you have to accept that the voice you just recorded is real.

There comes a time when you acknowledge what you've learned and then proceed to the next step. That's scientific, isn't it? Isn't that how it works? You advance in a systematic and methodical way, which makes it possible to believe in your data enough to carry on and see what happens. No? With many of these skeptics, you never see what comes next, because they refuse to see what just happened.

Well, it's true that just because I have recorded an EVP voice, it doesn't mean I am talking to a dead person, and there's no real way of knowing if it is a specific dead person. I might really want that to be my dad, for example, and the voice might even reinforce it, but there's no reason to believe the voice is being truthful. In fact, all I really know for sure is that there is a voice on the recorder – a voice that came from someone who wasn't there. It could be my father indeed, or an angel or a demon, or an alien or… Lord knows who else it could be, but I definitely can't claim it is anyone specific.

I really do understand the value of skepticism. I just don't understand the way we use its power. The role of skeptic isn't like being some kind of maniacal naysayer – it's not like faith, where you stand your ground because of a higher calling. Skepticism is an attitude marked by a tendency to doubt what others accept as true. That's all. There's nothing in that definition that suggests a skeptic has the authority of God Almighty to shoot down any idea that challenges another already established one.

Sometimes I find myself listening to EVP and doubt starts to creep in. I mean… that one voice sure does sound familiar, right? Sounds like it could be my own voice? Or maybe I am projecting – somehow sending my thoughts out there and causing the words in my subconscious to imprint on the recorder. Maybe it's not a spirit from another plane or dimension, but just my wicked and twisted thoughts being projected. Mental vomit formed permanently – digitally. Maybe I've just got it all wrong. I should dispense with all those EVP that raise questions. Sometimes, that's exactly what I do. If there's even a hint that the voice on the recorder can be logically explained, I do throw it out. But if not – I'm keeping it! And all the skeptics in the world aren't gonna talk me out of it. It doesn't take long before I find one that has the exact opposite effect – it so is not of this world that only a complete dolt would doubt it.

You know, I don't go into dark and abandoned mental hospitals in search of something to scare the bejesus out of me. I don't want to be scared. I don't like slasher movies, or any movie where demons take over anything. I don't want any cheap thrills or any roller coaster rides through hell. I get no satisfaction out of scaring little kids on Halloween; of pouncing from behind a closet door. I don't go on hay rides looking for the Headless Horseman, and if I can avoid hanging out in graveyards at night, I definitely will.

But I am not going to ignore a disembodied voice if it speaks to me. EVP have nothing to do with how smart anyone is, or how well they live their life, or how effective they are at work. EVP don't have much to do with anything for that matter. And you can't plan them, force them, or guarantee them, if the spirit wants to speak and be heard, then you'll hear them. And they don't have to justify themselves, perform scientifically, or suffer our immature attempts to dismiss them. It's my guess that there's free will wherever they are – free enough to reject the idea of making them do anything they're not inclined to do.

And I know there are people out there who take it all very seriously, who have a whole science involved. They only use Faraday boxes and they won't even attempt a session unless all noise and electrical/magnetic energy is well away from the environment. I know that, for some reason, scientific approaches must be employed if results are going to be accepted by the world at large.

But I maintain that it doesn't matter if the world accepts them. Truly, the world hasn't known about them for centuries upon centuries. It hardly matters whether society continues in this ignorant bliss about these kinds of spiritual matters. It's a shame, but some spiritual things are often shelved in the modern world. We like to think of ourselves as enlightened and informed, even if our enlightenment is superficial and misinformation rules the day.

And there's a problem with that, isn't there? Because if all you know is that there is a voice, then there is a vast amount you do not know. I am not one of those people who thinks that evil lurks around every corner; that there are demons in the breadbox or that Satan lives in my attic. Still, throughout all of recorded history there have been instances – credible, well-documented incidents – that indicate the intrusion of diabolical evil into our lives. I'm not referring to individuals like Hitler or Mao, or Wayne Gasey, Otis Toole or Charlie Manson. These people are evil enough, and we would be hard-pressed to find someone to disagree, but this is not the kind of evil that concerns me.

The evil that worries me cannot really be seen; finds its way inside of you and poisons everything about you. This kind of evil distorts whatever you feel and confounds your senses – takes over that which makes you who you are.

Evil is as surely a part of life as good – always has been, and for those who consider this to be a medieval attitude, look around. Has mankind improved over the millennia? Are we treating each other better or caring more for one another? With the genocide and ethnic cleansing we see, can we claim we've reached a higher calm toward one another? What do you recognize in hatred that remotely smacks of a finally evolved being? Certainly we wouldn't dare claim that we've progressed, would we?

A lot of questions to answer, but consider for a moment if we can answer any of those in the affirmative. It doesn't even take great insight to ascertain that mankind has taken two steps backward for every step forward. Christian scripture tells us that one day it will all end – that Jesus will come again and there will be a battle between ultimate good and ultimate evil. Surely, for those of us who believe in the truth of scripture, there can be no state of denial as to the goodness in mankind. If it must all come to an earned conclusion, then it is only logical to assume it's getting worse – not better.

I'm not a preacher, and I do not intend this to be a sermon, but to suggest that supreme evil is "under control" now that we're all so enlightened, is to show how poorly we know ourselves. Do we really strive for goodness, or do we merely over-emphasize and advertise those rare occasions when it surfaces. As a species, have we really progressed? Or have we perfected the rationalizations that cover our slide backward?

Think about it. Draw your own conclusions, but don't forget to ask yourself how well we exhibit love for one another. Is it present in the wars, or the in the starvation we only have to view from afar? Is our great love evident in the way we treat one another on a daily basis? And if not, then why not?

And the paranormal is no different. Under the cloak of language that defines such things, there is also evil in the paranormal. Many would say if it's not visible in the metaphorical "light of day," then it is darkness and in darkness lies evil. But attitudes such as this strip us of real understanding by shrouding our ability to learn with superstition and a vain protectiveness of the status quo. Surely everything paranormal is not bad, and most probably it's the same as what we already know – there is good, and there is evil.

The unfortunate thing is that when we step into the unknown, we don't know where we're stepping, and even those faint EVP voices could be spiritual landmines. To assume they are all representative of wonderful people we once loved is a mistake. They could be, but even if they are, are they exactly the same as when we knew them? Are they in heaven, or somewhere else? And why, if not in heaven? Does the soul remain the same soul we knew or does this new environment adjust it? And if the voices represent people, are they alone?

I think it is a very good idea to make the assumption that they are not alone. That somewhere in the mix of the next world, there are all kinds of energies – both good and evil – and all kinds of needs, wants, and passions. Making the profound conjecture that the entity behind the voices we capture as EVP are good souls full of love and longing for us, is a lot like stepping in front of a bullet.

I don't trust the voices, or put my faith in their words. I don't look to them for friendship or give them my confidence. I don't live my life according to their pontification or alter my course a single step due to their presence. There is nothing in an EVP from which we can learn about this life we live. We should study them and we should listen; try to learn what it is they teach us about their own existence, but under no circumstance should we elevate the voices to any status within our world. At the very least, they are deceased and have passed over to a different kind of animation. And it is always possible – always – that they are not and were never people, but instead, our wildest nightmares. We collate the data, and make best use of what we learn, but we never allow the voices to define, shape, or lead us.

It's easy for me – I've heard the voices. I've been there when they were recorded; I can defend the environment and I know the voices are real. I know that once the EVP has been properly scrutinized that I have heard from someone who does not fit our definition of alive. It no longer matters if my friends think it's funny; think I am spending too much time with it; think I'm weird, because when you finally understand what's going on, the old preconceived notions no longer count for much.

These voices are proof that God exists. They prove that there is an afterlife. There should be no more doubt about that. It's been shown that the most important promise has been kept. These voices make real the secret that there certainly is an entire supernatural world, and there's a really good chance it is populated by people we knew, and loved. People who were walking around last week perhaps; who loved us and cared for us when they were alive, are quite probably inhabiting that supernatural world. And it is so perfectly hidden that we will never ever find it, but we've caught a glimpse and we know it exists.

That's a lot to learn from a few EVP. Just words – with the most unusual origin ever. But these voices – these words - are like a Rosetta stone to the afterlife. They are the beginning - the first stages of something monumental. These voices are our first evidence.

And it doesn't matter who is behind the voice – friend or foe, relative or stranger, angel or demon – for now we know we're not alone. And knowing is most of the battle. Some might say our lives have meaning, because life after death is real. The skeptics won't be happy – they'll find newer and more convincing ways to show the masses that it's all a scam. And there will be many who will follow – most, probably. But not I.

I think the average person today wants his paranormal served up in 12 minute segments with commercials in between. I don't think the average person really wants to deal with the actual implications of real proof, or the ramifications possible with the unknown. Instead, they like their paranormal as entertainment; scary stories. Most of us want it left at that. Even people who admit they believe usually let it go at acceptance, and then distance. Lots of distance.

We want to go to the movies and be scared enough to forget all about it on the way home. We want our dead people to haunt the old mansion on the hill, and we want the heroine and her really smart friend to save us all from a rip in the fabric of time. That's the paranormal understanding most of us want – things we saw in the movies or on television. And it's all great fun. But it's not the truth - the truth is much different.

The truth is complex and not so terrible because it is God's truth. The truth requires faith. Not in the voices themselves, but faith that their existence attests to the creator's divine wisdom. Faith in the idea that it really is a perfectly orchestrated universe; faith in the covenant that on whatever constitutes the seventh day, He rested and that it was good.

Seek

I know we've all seen enough ghost hunting shows on television to realize that there are many different ways to handle an EVP session. Like most, I have generally used three basic methods. First is the one we're all most familiar with – the interview, where you ask the questions and hopefully the spirit answers or responds. Second – place the recorder nearby and record what goes on during the interim. And third, hide it somewhere before you even start the session – in your bag, or under a magazine, so that no one is aware that you are recording.

My best results have come from the second method. I like the idea of not asking questions but simply recording life as it goes on – primarily because I think spirits are more interested in watching us, and talking to one another about us, than they are in participating directly with us. Sometimes I even suspect that spirits are a little snobby – prefer not to engage in discourse unless it's unavoidable or instructive in some way. Of course, you don't always have a choice. Often you're the only living soul present, so you have to ask questions. Regardless, it doesn't matter. I've had good responses from all of these methods, and one should use whatever gets the job done – whatever you are most comfortable with at that moment.

Suggesting that there's only one way to do things – my way, or your way – isn't very smart. The right way is the one that yields results, so I only have one strict recommendation – never whisper. Most EVP are whispers or something very close – leave the whispering to the spirit. You're not going to be able to keep secrets from them anyway. Whatever you have to say should be said in a normal voice, and with a consistent attitude as well. You don't want to be unpleasant and loud one minute and then break out that agreeable "inside" voice a second later. It is my opinion that a consistent, even-keeled approach while recording EVP eliminates obstacles; delivers better results.

We don't know very much about spirits or how much they understand about the devices and methods we use during a session. Even though a digital recorder might be spectacularly small and quiet, spirits may well know exactly what it is. Personally, I think they're rather well educated for the most part – they know a lot more about how we chase them down than we think they do, so I would avoid reminding them how supposedly more advanced we are technologically. Just an opinion.

I am a huge proponent of treating spirits courteously. I personally don't think the aggressive, insulting approach works well, plus you typically get what you give. If you want a pissed off, unpleasant EVP, by all means say something really obnoxious. I wonder if there's anything we can learn from a pissed off spirit other than to reinforce the lack of common sense on our part. So, I like respect – a lot. I like the idea of being polite and saying hello – maybe introduce yourself. I have a feeling they know who you are anyway, but it's the civil thing to do, and I believe you catch more flies with honey.

Besides, I don't think treating a spirit like some kind of criminal is appropriate – especially if you embrace the 'hanging around" theory as I do. Just because someone was a real jackass in life doesn't mean he hasn't been shown the error of his ways in the afterlife. It seems a little shallow to assume that a spirit just picks up where he left off – pillaging, plundering and whatever. Certainly something could easily have jolted him into coming correct. That makes sense to me. Moving to the afterlife doesn't seem like a "ho hum' experience; there ought to be some sobering effect on one's attitude.

At any rate, the way I see it, I have the upper hand anyway. There are so few documented cases of a living person who has been harmed by a human spirit that being unpleasant to one has no real benefit. If you believe, like me, that there are probably entities everywhere all the time, then even if you're certain who you think you are addressing, you still can't know who else might be listening. There's nothing different about talking to a spirit than to anyone else, and I honestly cringe when I see an investigator get all rude and pushy for no apparent reason. I've heard it is done to guarantee better results, but that sounds like an excuse to assert oneself. And it seems as if that sort of approach is suggesting that the spirits should be obligated to talk to us, or at the very least, are stupid enough to be so crudely manipulated into communicating. Do we suddenly become moronic and unable to control our impulses when we pass away into the afterlife?

Sometimes I don't understand why investigators are so sold on the idea that in a place purported to be haunted, the spirit in question is trapped there. We don't know that. I guess if we were capturing photos and video showing entities that looked like particular people, we could make a claim like that. But unless I'm missing something, there is very little proof as to the actual identity of most ghosts. I mean, its great story-telling, and far be it from me to squeeze the fun out of a good ghost story, but an investigation is not the place for developing tall tales. And a serious EVP session shouldn't be wrapped up with guesswork and "what ifs."

One particular television show always follows the playing of their EVP by asking the question "could this be…?" And even though they're a bit too dramatic for my taste, I like that part. It indicates the truth of the EVP and suggests a possible explanation for that truth while leaving an understanding that nothing is chiseled in stone.

Paranormal investigators usually mention the three types of hauntings – interactive, residual, and poltergeists –

and I wouldn't dare disagree with that. But the key word here is haunted. If someplace is haunted, then by definition it is inhabited or regularly visited by a ghost or a supernatural being. Anyway, I'm not going to talk about what makes a house haunted because there are a ton of people with more credentials than I. But for me, the interactive haunt, while most interesting, can often be confusing. Mixing in the "hanging around" theory, you would almost have to conclude that every place is haunted. I mean, logically, if the deceased are free to move about, then they would predictably be present practically everywhere.

As a result, I don't believe that capturing an EVP necessarily means a place is continually or permanently haunted. The spirit belonging to the voice might belong there, but it could also simply be passing through or visiting. If you accept the notion that these voices are coming from people who might be sharing our space and time while occupying another dimension or plane, then they might not be haunting anything in our reality. They could be exactly where they are supposed to be. The fact that they can still interact with us, especially through EVP, does not automatically scream haunting to me. In fact, it could be a property of the afterlife to be aware of us and able to interact to some degree.

Also, we tend to think of spirits as being right there with us, but there's really nothing to suggest that's the case either. In fact, as far as EVP are concerned, I think it is hardly ever the case. I think they're somewhere else completely. They could be in another dimension, or they could be residing in an astral plane, or they could be in a place we cannot begin to detect, see or imagine.

There are so many possibilities – primarily because we have no actual proof as yet. They may seem as if they're part of earth's population in some strange way, but trying to ascertain that is too impossible. I have always figured that if they were a part of our existence, then they wouldn't be so hard to spot; wouldn't have to manifest themselves. As part of this world, they would absolutely have shape and form of some kind – shape and form that would be consistent with everything we are used to for a living entity. They would have weight and dimension, require sustenance - even something to stave off infection. They cannot be part of our environment.

In our environment, life does not shape-shift or disappear at will. If entities were to actually occupy space of some kind in our world, use and radiate energy, then how could the universe we are all a part of include the presence of so many souls? It would be like we were the outsiders – not them – and we very clearly are in charge around here. They, are from somewhere else.

Practically everyone understands a residual haunting – it's like a recording, playing out events that happened in the past involving individuals who are long since gone. There's no evidence that a residual haunt actually represents a spirit presence at all, and there are many who suggest it definitely does not. And poltergeist activity is a rather heated subject since there are many who feel that a poltergeist is actually projection from living beings. Paranormal, definitely, but then does this really classify as a haunting if it is generated from one of us?

But an interactive haunt is so incredibly unique. By its very name, we consider this as a true haunting, even in the Hollywood sense. The spirit knows where they are, understands who we are. There are goals in mind for everyone involved, and the spirit elects to interact with us. But I have heard well-known investigators indicating that the spirit is somehow limited and isolated within the house, and I wonder about the wisdom of such a statement. I think I prefer to think of it as a spirit who frequently returns to an area for reasons understood only by him or her. That might be sucking the fun out of things, but I think it's a more accurate characterization.

Why would a spirit pass away, assume the delineations assigned to the afterlife, but figure a way to remain physically tied to an earthly existence? Especially when the physical science of their world and ours are not – can not be - compatible. If they were somehow able to remain here – if a spirit was able to move freely through our world, then there is no reason we couldn't duplicate their behavior for ourselves. For instance, if it were really possible for our energy and essence to float in an ectoplasmic cloud, then it should only be a matter of time before we figure out a way to do just that on our own. Spiritual entities said to manifest in such a way do so because they exist in a place where such things are possible. We just don't understand the how and why of it yet.

There is no such thing as an undead, or a person who is deceased but doesn't actually leave. That energy manifests itself in some other way than life as we experience it, and the things we see and hear may seem to be developing in our physical world, but there has to be another explanation. Besides, in all religions, God promises the afterlife – he guarantees it for both the righteous and the evil among us. There is always an end to our mortal coil. It seems sloppy of any god to go to all the trouble of creating specific versions of an afterlife only to allow a loophole for certain souls. After all, one thing is common among all faiths – God is smarter than us, and His justice is pure. As far as I'm concerned, a pure sense of justice doesn't allow for any percentage of sloppiness. There is no leniency from death – it takes us all, and God's justice is swift and accurate. When your time is up, you die. There are no pacts with the devil or ancient voodoo potions. We have to believe that God is in control and wins this battle – death is guaranteed to every last one of us; and while there are certainly many things we can do to prolong our lives, we all meet our end by and by. So, the idea of trapped souls doesn't seem as if God has done a very good job at handing out that justice.

Mind you, I totally believe in ghosts and spirits and all of that, but not the part about them being attached to any piece of our physical world. I also accept the criticism of those who are already tired of my religious interjections.

But as I see things, it is becoming more and more acceptable to keep religion out of the paranormal as if it is some sort of false barometer that prevents mankind from progressing in any kind of spiritual direction. Nonsense.

Mankind has always had religion, and we always will. It's not even about whether or not our religion of choice is the "right" religion. It is about the need for humans to practice religion – to find a way to fuse the supernatural and the natural world into some kind of cohesive survival mechanism. We need religion almost as much as we need to eat and breathe. Many people won't agree with that, but if you extrapolate the idea that religion is a strongly held set of beliefs, values and attitudes, then I think you would also agree that religion is fused into every aspect of life, on a daily basis, and comes to the forefront as soon as we need it. An individual's religious belief could be as unique as he or she is, or it could be as structured as the denominational dogma we have all been exposed to. If standard religion is not acceptable, people will invent something on their own to take its place without even realizing it.

In all probability, a spirit is either moving at tremendous speeds, or is not restricted by time. After all, who is to say that linear time applies at all in the afterlife. It could be that occupants of the afterlife are able to be in more than one place at the same time, or able to travel at the speed of light, fold space, or something completely unthought of by any of us.

So, I strongly and seriously doubt that linear time applies

to the spirit world at all. They come and go in the blink of an eye, and have no sense of passing time. I believe that to a spirit, yesterday has no relation to today whatsoever. Imagine spending eternity doing anything? How could you do it without going totally bonkers or, at the very least, getting royally bored? Time couldn't possibly be an issue for the spirits – they can probably go back in time if they like, or forward. To them, our entire lives could seem like a minute if they deem it so, or they could relive things they loved over and over, lingering in the emotion of a single second for years at a time – drinking in the passion and the feelings that second generates within them – over and over. At the same instant, they could travel anywhere around, through or within our earth.

Someone who fits this description is not a creature that simply haunts a house – why would they when they don't have to? And if they are haunting the place for whatever reason, there is no rationale to assume that they are trapped, as if that's all they can be or do. If living humans are granted our free will as we languish at the bottom of the spiritual totem pole, why do we assume a transformed soul has absolutely none? No, I don't see this entity as a creature who only haunts a house. Entities, such as we will all become, live a life of some kind and probably visit our world whenever it suits them. And if there truly is a haunting, one with enough evidence, I would suggest we consider that it may not be a full-time job for those doing the haunting.

But maybe I should relate this to EVP, since that's what

I am supposed to know about. It doesn't matter how many good EVP you capture at a location, if the location is haunted, those EVP need to hands-down support whatever other evidence has been gathered. Otherwise, while interesting, their value is incidental.

In the case of my mother's house, for instance, there has never been any conclusive evidence captured anywhere in the home. Some very minor things, yes, but nothing categorical enough to constitute a haunting. There are no manifestations, apparitions, or shadow people; no books flying off shelves; no unexplained banging in the attic. In short, my mother's house is extremely peaceful, and gives not one single vibe of being haunted. Still, the woman's house has some serious EVP going on – always. That in itself convinces me that the "hanging around" theory is correct – the house is visited, constantly. There are a lot of voices who drop by, and they have been recorded, but these constitute the only evidence of a haunting. Without the knowledge of EVP, no one would presume to label the house as such, and yet, the presence of so many voices does just that. How many other homes, businesses and buildings might be the same? My guess is – most.

I have recorded some kind of EVP at every location where I've tried. Now, I can hear the disbelief rising out there at making such a statement, but it's true. Certainly it could be possible that spirits seek me out, and that has even been suggested by more than one sensitive, but it is also feasible that it happens because the hereafter allows for such access to our world.

Since I am primarily concerned with EVP, and since that is where my investigative experience lies, I feel that I have enough background in the area to suggest that EVP constitute the best and most prolific substantiation gathered in the field. However, while EVP are definitely paranormal, they can't be considered ghosts in the same way we traditionally think of ghosts, unless we are prepared to change our definition. They might very well be that, but there are too many other explanations of who or what they possibly are. One of those is an angel. I have recorded some voices that sound quite different from the rest, and they always comment in a way that seems profoundly peaceful and helpful. I started believing right away that these occasional voices were indeed the voices of angels who, for some reason, decided to be heard. Can we suggest that angels – the messengers of God - are haunting a house? I don't think so.

Of course, labeling an EVP as an angel is not easily done. In spite of my feelings or certainties, an angel is way too special. Scripture states that angels are representatives of God and have done His bidding throughout all of time. An angel visited Mary with news of her virgin pregnancy, for God's sake. I have a lot of trouble assigning that kind of importance to an EVP no matter how much I believe it in my heart.

I once had occasion to watch a man go into a convenience store and unsuccessfully try to borrow money from everyone inside. Looking dejected and definitely empty-handed, he came outside to me as I was sitting on the hood of my car waiting for a friend. He asked me for money to buy milk for his children, so I reached in my pocket and offered him all I had – a five dollar bill. The man stopped me, put his hand close to my face and said, "No. You will be blessed." And with that, he disappeared - right before my eyes. I was forced to divert my eyes for only a fraction of a second, and when I looked back up, he was nowhere in sight.

Was my panhandling friend an angel? Scripture suggests that we might just be tested from time to time, so he could have been. Certainly every person I have ever told the story to has believed that this guy was an angel, and I agree. But do I know that? No. And there will never be a shred of evidence to sustain such a claim. Literally everyone may be convinced, but that is based totally on faith – the evidence is not there. And because of my beliefs, I hope I am never so arrogant to claim angelic presence because of an EVP.

Of course, all of this is fodder for the theorists. I think the common wisdom is that an EVP voice is the voice of the individual supposed to be haunting the location. So the recorded voice gets designated as belonging solely to the ghost being hunted, and sometimes that very well may be exactly accurate, but not always. I am certain from listening to EVP that there are transient voices chiming in from time to time - a friend we forgot about, unknown family, friends of family, interested parties, passersby, lower demons. If we make the assumption that the presence of an EVP indicates a haunting by a particular spirit, we might be labeling a lot of places inaccurately. So, in order for an EVP to support a haunting, there has to be other evidence that strongly suggests a tie to that EVP. Otherwise, the EVP is just a voice; paranormal and possibly linked to people and places present, but nothing more.

For me, the EVP is, more often than not, disassociated with any actual activity that happens at a location. For the most part, EVP are less than spectacular during an investigation because they are so difficult to directly tie to other evidence. When I started doing this, I expected the EVP to be full of ghostly references and complaints about wherever the spirit found itself. I expected EVP to have an agenda of sorts – goals, perhaps; items the voice wanted accomplished. I was also positive that EVP had to belong wherever they were found. But there's no accurate way to assign a goal or a location. I'm not even completely certain that the entity belonging to a voice knows any more about things than we do.

Consider this: The vast majority of EVP I have captured consist of two or more different voices talking together – usually commenting on what the living are actually doing at the time. They speak to one another the way we converse during a movie or a television show. Isn't it possible that those EVP do not represent an attempt by the voices in question to communicate to us at all; that they might be accidental; that maybe the voices have no idea they are being heard?

We have always thought that an EVP resulted from spirit

interaction with our world in order to be heard, but since we don't really know how any of this is accomplished, it is just as likely to be us, and our technology, that punches through the veil. The fact that we don't know we're doing it wouldn't be surprising, would it? After all, we're the hunters. It is we who want to make a profound connection to the unknown – perhaps we have found a way that we are unaware of at this point in our quest.

I have had very few EVP that had an ax to grind. I would estimate that less than ten percent of them are critical of anything or want to see any type of action undertaken. Most of what I have heard has been in the form of comment – usually about us, and not usually directed to us. My experience is that they aren't typically singular travelers – they come in couples or groups. They talk to one another and we can hear them respond in kind. I have recorded more than a few EVP that ridicule us in some way. They seem as if they're on the other side of a one-way mirror, watching intently, poking fun, making affirmative comments when they agree with us, and negative ones when they don't. They enjoy swearing now and again, but it isn't as prevalent as what I've heard from the living.

And every once in awhile, an EVP will talk directly to me – sometimes calling me by name. I've had them tell me to stop smoking – often. They've told me they were "dead" several times. EVP have commented on the food I am eating – from chocolate (a favorite everywhere, apparently) to chicken and cherry pie. They speak of family and love occasionally, and sometimes they make political comments. They mention the temperature every now and then, and have admitted to ringing my doorbell, setting off my smoke detector, and making my dog go crazy.

They're not always the most eloquent speakers in the universe, limiting themselves to a few words, but when they really want to get a point across, there has been no doubt. By far, the vast majority of the hundreds of EVP I have been able to capture sound like everyday people – the recordings are like snapshots of specific moments in their existence. It would be easy to want to name them and associate them with people we loved and missed, and since they seem to possess personalities, it's tempting to match them to our lives in some way. Most of my EVP are friendly, engaged, likable, funny, and intelligent. They are thoughtful souls who have opinions and beliefs.

But there are some EVP which are obviously none of the above. They're nasty and frequently suggest some really awful stuff. They tell you to go "fuck yourself," make vile racial comments, and insult you. Now I realize that these could be manifestations of formerly human souls that have simply amplified the kind of people they were in life. Perhaps these are transient spirits – maybe Hitler and Himmler were strolling by one day and felt the need to disrespect the Jews one more time. Or some deceased murderer found himself listening in and decided to throw some prison language into the fray. There's no reason to think transient spirits are always going to be nice. There's no reason to think that only people in "heaven" are available to comment. Since we don't know what their world looks like to them, there's no telling what kind of environmental conditions are influencing these comments. I suppose if you were looking at a barren hellscape day after year after century, you might not have continued to encourage your more sensitive qualities.

And even more distasteful is the possibility that these marauding nasties were never from this world, but demonic in nature. Now I can't comment on demons except to say that there is scripture in every religion that accounts for them. Fallen angels… whatever you want to call them, it is a real possibility that these guys are available for comment as well. Who's to say they're not? We don't know one way or the other, so I think it behooves us to watch out or, at the very least, take care enough not to engage such creatures or invite them over for tea. These miscreants have never had an earthly history; were never human – so their place is most certainly not with us. These guys are bad news no matter how you dice it.

Getting too involved with bad entities is a real likelihood for anyone doing any kind of paranormal research or investigation. It may not happen often, but it does happen. Indeed, it is by far the only explanation of what has invaded the lives of some people. There may not be that many provable cases of possession, but if there is a single one, that one bears strong enough witness against purposely inviting any involvement. People can accidentally attract a demon whenever they seek to communicate with spiritualized entities. It's the whole Ouija Board scenario. If you ask someone not of this realm to come forward, who's to say what will take you up on the offer.

I would strongly suggest that EVP not be treated as a parlor game under any circumstance. This is no way to entertain oneself whenever bored people get together. Contacting the supernatural is not something you just do for the thrill of it – it can be dangerous, and you can be saddled with misery for a very long time. It is stone-cold guaranteed that one minute spent with hell's misfits is one minute too long. Paranormal training of some kind – knowledge and a historical perception, should be the prerequisite for any EVP session. In short, don't be stupid. Don't open doors you will not be able to close. Investigate, yes – carefully.

But then there is the other side of the coin. I am completely convinced that in order to record EVP, you need to be open to it. That's not to say it can't happen otherwise, but if you believe there are voices, and if you believe you can record them, your odds of being successful at it go way up. If someone expresses an interest in you, aren't you more receptive to hearing what they have to say? If you know that you are respected, aren't you more likely to express even controversial opinions? So why would a spirit be any different? It's like being a magnet, and your power of attraction makes you desirable to speak to. Since EVP can show up on one recorder and not on another in the same place, then there is obviously some selection process going on. Perhaps the guy most open to it all gets the reward.

I don't think the typical EVP voice represents an entity that is ignorant of too many things by comparison to us. I think it's reasonable to assume their world is more advanced than ours. If nothing else, it would seem to be more expansive. If the afterlife represents a transcendence from human existence, then it is only logical that the afterlife holds more possibilities within it.

But this is all speculation, and in practical terms, it is my contention that the spirit world is less interested in our world than we think. To a spirit, we have to appear primitive and oppressed by linear time, so why would a more advanced being care? There has to be something interesting enough about us to attract even the smallest amount of attention. Perhaps it's loved ones left behind, or the things a spirit might miss from the earth. But regardless, I think that if we exhibit the advanced thought that the supernatural is as real as the natural; if we are open to understanding things we can only imagine - perhaps that openness wins us a temporary spot at the table and they throw us a bone from time to time. Being open to knowledge usually develops understanding. Being open to possibilities usually develops knowledge. And by becoming a more spiritually diverse and malleable being, I think we become more interesting to them. The seeker finds. Those who never seek, never do.

The King James version of the Bible tells us in Proverbs 25:2 that "It is the glory of God to conceal a thing: but the honour of kings is to search out a matter." This concept runs throughout all religions, but the meaning is clear in each of them. It is God's business to hide whatever He pleases from us – it is His will that matters, and His reasons are part of His wisdom. But He is giving us permission to seek. In fact, scripture calls it our "honor" to do so, and so we should. Being open to questions is the best first step to finding the answers.

But how is it likely to be open to possibilities that potentially include the demonic and intense negativity? How can I say on one hand to be cautious and steer clear of the dreadful, but be open to communicating with the unknown? It's obviously one of those slippery slopes, and there is no rule of thumb or fail-safe answer to that question. I think that part of being open to spirits is to pay attention to them; hear what they are saying; read between as many lines as you can. And never become obsessed with it. Any kind of paranormal investigation can become addictive, but always keep things in perspective and give your life and the people in it the top priority always.

There was a time when I began to feel extremely uneasy about the EVP I was collecting. Some things were said during the sessions that made my skin crawl. If someone had spoken like that face to face, it might not have been so frightening, but the idea that a spirit went out of its way to say those things, made me wonder just who it was I was recording and talking to. I felt I needed guidance.

I tried to contact everyone I could think of with a history of dealing with EVP; anyone in the paranormal community I'd ever read about, listened to, or watched on television – including all manner of famous people and groups. I figured that since they had websites and email addresses, they would respond in time, and answer my questions or offer advice. In some cases, I left several emails, and with regard to one particularly famous group of investigators, I wrote to everyone on the team. I'd hoped to get some help, of course, so I made sure to indicate my level of distress.

No one ever responded. Not a single word. When I cried out for help, no one cared. My fear turned into frustration, and I began thinking that perhaps these high-profile individuals were fakes, mere entertainers. It made me feel stupid for even thinking I had recorded legitimate EVP in the first place. These paranormal investigators were nothing more than a public relations package, or a character in a script. I was angry!

And I won't go on and on and initiate any of the usual rancor and slop against anyone who gains notoriety. It's part of the cult of personality to both love these people and hate them, so I choose not to do either. I also turned to several religious orders – United Methodist, Catholic, Episcopalian, Metaphysical and Jewish. No one was interested there either. A couple of them feigned curiosity and promised to help me understand what was happening; said they would get back to me with resources, but they never did. I am totally certain that they all marked me as a nut case, placating my delusions as they sent me on my way – probably praying that I would forget all about them.

I continued to record and capture EVP, but I became very suspicious of everything, and I refused to engage in a session unless I felt in control of it. I listened to my inner voice every time from that point on, and it made me extremely cautious, which is a good thing.

Finally, I started emailing local paranormal or investigative groups and eventually, a local group answered my email. The founder and I talked for hours about what I was going through, and the bottom line is they even did an investigation of my mother's house. I was allowed to participate, and eventually joined the team.

That aside, were it not for them, I would still be "alone" out there. I guess the point of even mentioning this is to let you know that any kind of paranormal investigation – whether under the auspices of an established and well-equipped group, or alone in your basement with nothing but a Sony digital recorder – can be dangerous. Don't take chances, go with your feelings, act naturally, and stay focused on what's truly important in life.

I began looking for EVP during the day, at my mother's house, and I only recorded during times I would normally have been there. Most of the EVP sessions at my own home were done at night during the same period. I don't think the time of day matters. I realize that most investigations happen at night – but as far as my EVP are concerned, I actually prefer daylight hours. I have also noticed that the quantity of voices seems to increase on overcast days, although I don't have actual statistics. This is just the way it turned out for me, but I think it's a really good idea to record at all different times of day. I think any life force has preferences or periods of down time, and that may be a governing factor as to what sort of results you get.

I am also of the opinion that the voices like consistency. If there is a particular voice that you have a history with, and if it thinks you will be recording at noon all the time, I think there is a good chance it will be there at that time more often than not. One experiment of mine that I call my Doorbell Project was designed to have a definite meet time between 12:00 and 1:00. If either one of us wanted to talk, we would do it then. This particular entity was a doorbell ringer, and that was my signal to get the recorder and begin a session. The voice took ownership of ringing the doorbell, but had the disarming habit of ringing it at all times of day - usually when I was completely unable to make the right effort. The doorbell would ring when I was cooking dinner, or in the middle of Survivor (which I would not miss), and invariably it would visit while everyone in the house was making noise. This is no way to run an EVP session, so I decided to try a compromise with the spirit.

I told him that I would make that time available every day. He could ring the doorbell when he wanted to talk, or I would just start a session during that time when I wanted to talk. Surprisingly enough, the doorbell stopped ringing by itself during odd times. Even now, it almost always rings during the noon hour as I requested, and when it does, we immediately begin a session. At first, these sessions were very fruitful, yielding twice as many EVP as was usual for the location. But that began to slow down – perhaps his enthusiasm waned, or perhaps his own schedule was not suited to my parameters. Eventually, the doorbell stopped ringing on a regular basis, although there are occasional sparsely spaced events.

Likewise, whenever I was the one to call the meeting, so to speak, there were very few responses – some days, there was no one there at all. I'm not entirely sure what to make of it either, but I still have some random EVP from time to time, even though the interactive conversations we were beginning to enjoy seem to have vanished. I don't think that voice liked being asking for a name as frequently as I asked, and I may have annoyed him by doing it. I actually asked if he was ready to give me a name several times, and on at least two occasions, he said he wouldn't do it, so I've stopped asking.

Interestingly, I never got an outward response, though I always asked for one. I requested two knocks to indicate his presence – any kind of knocks or taps, but I never heard them. However, there are frequent double clicks on the recorder that sound like they are flaws in the machine of some kind, and they always accompany my request. Of course, this tells me he is manipulating the recorder just as the professional ghost hunters have always said. For whatever reason, this spirit is either too weak to affect the natural world, or he doesn't want to. I have found him to be very independent in the past, and he never responds just to please me. This is, of course, his right, and I have never tried to badger or provoke him into doing what I want instead.

Worth noting, that the sessions I have been referring to are all daytime sessions at my home. The evening sessions there seemed to take on a whole other ambience. It was during these interviews at night that I began hearing the nastiness which caused me to seek guidance (as I mentioned earlier). I would hesitate to draw any conclusions as to the time of day and the attitude of the spirit, but I do believe that they were different voices. And it felt a lot as if the evening spirits had nothing to do with their daytime counterpart – almost as if they were unaware of one another. Pure conjecture, of course, but suffice it to say that there was activity all around the clock.

I have always felt that it is better to let the EVP speak for themselves. It might not be surprising that most people flat out don't believe me. I never try to hide my interest in the subject and I always mention that I have a great many samples to prove that EVP really do exist, but I am quite proficient at spotting "the look." And I get it a lot. So I do wish it were possible for everyone to listen to the voices I have recorded and then make up their mind. I suppose it's easier to close our minds than it is to believe there are unseen beings which are actually able to communicate with us.

I don't know why the average person suddenly becomes an uber skeptic, but they seem to. There are all sorts of automatic responses – each one aimed at proving how stupid I am to believe the voices are generated by spirits. It's as if I haven't a brain in my head, because they have the answer almost immediately. If I were bright enough, I too could have figured it out as quickly as they did. They realize this a subject they know nothing about, but they still have rationale and explanations for why it's not possible. For some reason, it's all too provocative for them to allow me to continue thinking what I have recorded is real. I'm sure there was a time when I'd have been labeled a heretic, or worse, so perhaps I should count myself lucky.

Maybe it is a subject too religious in nature, and it offends their sense of God and what's right and wrong – like maybe my voices are from Satan, and if I were a better Christian I would cease immediately, and ask for forgiveness. I've actually been told that once – almost verbatim. Some others seem to feel that I've watched too many paranormal television shows, and I'm just incredibly silly and stupid for not realizing it is all bogus and just for fun – like a Steven King film. I've also had people request to hear the voices, and then spend great amounts of time trying to get me to tell them how I did it. They just don't believe it's real, and I would guess… people like that never will.

But there are others who do believe, and many of those are completely creeped out by it all. Of course, that's not the goal of an EVP session, and sometimes it disturbs me to think my voices have upset someone, or worse, frightened them. I have a nephew in Chicago who had trouble sleeping for a few days after listing to the EVP on my website. He heard all the voices, had no doubts, and found himself pondering whether or not these spirits were visiting his home as well. "That one sounded like Poppop" and if Poppop could hang out in my house, he could come to Chicago in a heartbeat. As much as he loved his Poppop, my father, he needed to feel secure the man was in the ground and not haunting anyone. Unfortunately for my nephew, I recorded EVP in his house while on a visit. And he was in the room at the time.

I guess you'd have to conclude that reactions to EVP are very diverse, and the voices become instantly controversial. People who know nothing about it at all jump to all sorts of conclusions very quickly, and most of the time these conclusions are negative. Whether the EVP are fakes, stupid delusions on my part, or come straight from hell, people who react negatively do so without even an ounce of desire to know the truth. I don't think it actually matters, but in turn, it makes me wonder about a few things myself.

I wonder why someone would dismiss evidence in such an arbitrary and off-handed way. I wonder why it is more important to protect their status quo than it is to know the truth. And I wonder how we can come to fear so quickly and without good reason. I know the standard response when I ask those questions, and I know that it's human nature to be guarded and resistant to change, but this is supposedly an advanced civilization and mankind has never been so well educated. I wish I could, but I doubt I will ever be able to completely get it – attitudes from the Dark Ages should have stayed in the Dark Ages.

For me, an EVP is a revelation. It is important! It's every bit as significant as a flying saucer would be. Can you imagine what would happen if we were suddenly faced with proof that little green men did actually exist and were visiting regularly? Such an event would change the course of human history in a major way. For me, EVP are the same. The very existence of this kind of evidence excites me beyond any ability to describe – I am suddenly privy to a secret of the universe so dynamic and significant that my entire attitude toward life has to be different as a result.

Good Lord! Mankind has been spouting off about ghosts and spirits for thousands of years, and now... here is proof. A voice from somewhere we cannot see. A voice that we cannot naturally hear, from someone we classify as no longer alive. That seems like such amazing stuff to me – earth-shattering and mind-altering stuff. There ought to be research projects funded, and experiments performed with a never ending supply of newly developed equipment. There ought to be NASA-like government agencies aimed at learning as much as possible... But alas, as of now, EVP are just silly voices from Neverland that should challenge us to learn, but are summarily dismissed and predominantly ignored instead.

"It is the glory of God to conceal a thing: but the honour of kings is to search out a matter." It seems to me that this is a call to arms. We are being outright challenged to seek the truth with God's blessing; to look under every rock for any essence of new knowledge. I firmly believe God gave us vibrant and vigorous intellects to find ways to improve and expand our consciousness. Great achievements have been the norm on our planet – diseases cured, scientific challenges made real, dreams realized, fears conquered… We've traveled to the moon, gazed at the peaks of Titan through the lens of a camera millions of miles away… We've proven to ourselves time and time again that we're adaptable and resourceful, but now we're faced with intense environmental issues that will test our clarity of vision and our will to survive. Do we care enough to end world hunger, or genocide and ethnic cleansing? Or pestilence, stronger and more resistant bacteria, racial hatred… the theocratic control of our insight and thoughts…

Now is certainly not the time to retard our thinking and close our minds to the potential we embody, or the chance of deepening our spiritual awareness and transcending the business-as-usual way of the world. Instead of plodding along living lives of distraction and uncertainty, we should be learning – always learning – and growing; seeking the answers to our eternal questions and finding God's truth. Truly, mankind will advance and mankind will regress – it's always been that way, but the goal should be to travel as close to the light as possible, not to hide in the shadows nurturing our fears and feeding ignorance.

Were I a physicist, I would be extolling our obligation to delve deeper into particle theory; a doctor – the necessity of stem cell research. But this is a book about EVP and the paranormal – a subject even less accepted and even more forgotten amid the challenges of expanding our horizons. So it seems to me that we will learn more about who and what we are as paranormal studies continue throughout the ages – hopefully, without the myopic fear and mistrust that has traditionally accompanied the subject; remembering that as the scripture teaches, it is our honor to seek. This honor bestowed upon us by God Himself – confirmation that seeking truth is every bit as important as finding it.

Magnet

I've been able to record a lot of EVP. This is not something I boast about, or even something I count as a skill. It just so happens that when I turn on my recorder I am able to capture disembodied voices, and by most standards, the quantity and quality of them is fairly high. I have plenty of voices that would not stand up very well to a skeptic's litmus test as to what is or is not paranormal; voices that are muddy and distant; whispers that sound a lot like someone sighing in the background. I try my best to eliminate those because as far as I'm concerned, if an EVP can be easily "shot down," then it can't be evidence, and evidence is what floats my boat. The only EVP I am interested in keeping are those which cannot be explained or attributed to anything earthly.

There's no reason for me to make the efforts I've made to hear these voices if they can't stand up to debunking. It's not something I do only because it's fun. I can think of a hundred things more entertaining than listening over and over to time I just lived. I do this because I believe they are voices from beyond and that the EVP I record will add to the collective body of evidence being gathered worldwide in the paranormal field. And if experts in the field wish to discount all of my EVP save one, then I consider it a success. A solitary piece of irrefutable evidence is a powerful thing, and I would be more than pleased to have contributed in even the smallest way.

That said, I believe I have recorded many voices, and unfortunately, they don't tell me very much. Certainly nothing about heaven and hell, or how to live my life. They don't convict or absolve me of my sins, nor do they let me in on little secrets about the great beyond. I have heard there are others whose EVP do all of these things and more, but mine do not. My EVP are just voices. They come in all shapes and sizes; can be soft and almost lost; loud and in your face. They seem to be individuals with personalities, and can be identified as such. I cannot control these voices or manipulate them into performing. They seem to have their own will and therefore do and say pretty much whatever they like. They ask nothing of me and pay absolutely no mind to almost everything I ask of them.

There are others in the field who hear things I cannot hear, and they claim to be able to use this information to lead so-called earthbound souls to the light. They hear entire conversations, receive instructions, and carry out wishes from the other side. My EVP don't do any of that. And quite honestly, if an EVP told me to do something, it would fall on deaf ears, because I wouldn't really know whose bidding I'd be doing. I have always seen my role in this whole paranormal thing as limited – as a seeker of knowledge, if you will. I want to learn and discover and further the knowledge base – the lack of which seems to suffocate paranormal discovery. And I think it is my duty to pursue any avenue that reveals truth in this area, but I won't be doing chores for the spirit world.

Supernatural entities do not have control over me. It is my belief that I also have a free will and make my own decisions, speak my own mind, and live my own life. If God Almighty wants to reach me, whether through an angel or whatever, I am certain He will do so in a way that is both convincing and uncontroversial. So, no, I am not interested in finding the answers to spiritual philosophies from the speakings of disembodied voices. In a strange way, EVP are very much like protozoa in a Petri dish to me – they merit study and elicit the need for understanding. They represent a piece of a very complex puzzle, and if I have been blessed with adding to the solution in some way, then I will count myself fortunate and useful.

Mind you, this is not to criticize those who see it differently. I can't judge another's experience in this domain any more than I can dismiss whatever they offer. But I know in my heart that if God wanted me to do His bidding, there would be no question about the request. He knows it would take much more than even the best Class A disembodied voice to get my obedience.

So, I am a listener. I'm not one of those paranormal thrill

seekers who live, eat and breathe the stuff. Well, I do spend a lot of time recording and listening, analyzing and culling, but there are many other things in life that occupy my time. And it is my hope to learn more about the paranormal in general over the rest of my years on this side of the curtain, but I will always place the living of my life as first. Learning about the paranormal, searching for answers to the thousands of unanswered questions, has only a fraction to do with the kind of person I am continually growing to become, and my EVP do not define me as a human being.

Outside of EVP, I haven't had a lot of experiences with the spirit world – not so far. I've seen a couple of things, but there was always an explanation of sorts – something cogent enough to cause me to doubt my senses. I once thought I saw my father standing at the thermostat one winter night, but by the time I looked back, he was gone. I don't believe he was really there – even now. I think it was something I had in my head at the time, and for just a brief second or two, I saw what I was thinking. Right after he passed away, I saw him enter the bedroom and ask me if "everything was alright?" I replied that it was and watched him walk out the bedroom door. I followed just a second later, but he was gone. I have always believed that was a dream.

My only experience with a ghost seems to have involved the same person in the same house. Never happened with any other deceased relatives – just dad, and I suppose that's explainable as well, since his passing was still fresh, and I had yet to grieve. Even though I can still see both of those images as clear as if they were yesterday, I have convinced myself that they're both inaccurate and figments of my imagination. But you know, they make for great experiences, so at least there's that, even without evidence.

But not too long ago, something else happened to me, and I bring it up here to hopefully make a point or two. I'd been doing EVP for a few months and had even successfully recorded some very interesting high quality voices at the local graveyard. At the time, I wasn't enthusiastic to engage with spirits I didn't know - I was still under the impression that the voices I'd captured up to then were family members. So the idea of strangers made me a little uneasy.

But this graveyard and I were old friends. I prefer to call them graveyards; much better than the other names, and it is descriptive and to the point. Graveyards are places to warehouse our dead; somewhere to put the bodies of our lives. We visit the day of the funeral and on special holidays… sometimes. Maybe we show up on an anniversary for a few minutes, pausing only briefly, wearing our best somber expression and the sad resignation that one day, we will be deposited there as well.

We shake our heads and say "she was so young," or we try to remember what it was that he meant to us. Glimpses of her face flicker in our minds; perhaps an elusive and fleeting hint of who she was dances in and out of the picture as we struggle with the certainty of death and vow to keep the memory more faithfully alive in the future. We are aware that this, too, is our own resting place one day, and we try to lessen that horror with a quick prayer and an even quicker exit.

Lore suggests that the dead wander these places at dark, and tales tell of encounters with the deceased on moonlit nights when shadows roam through the headstones and hide in the crypts – poised to lunge at whatever living thing passes by. He who goes to the graveyard in the dark, it is rumored, may not live to tell the horrors that await us all.

Even so, we all know such notions to be nothing more than stories. Has anyone really failed to survive a cemetery visit? What evidence proves that mysterious and evil ghouls wander there as if alive, hell-bent on wreaking ruin and harm to all who enter? This defies the very nature of a resting place, and surely all the fables of twisted grave robbers and demented gatekeepers are nothing more than fiction.

But Druid Ridge is my graveyard of choice. I go there to photograph the beauty of the place. Druid Ridge Cemetery defies all those dark and sinister notions. There are no toppled markers from past centuries; no tangled underbrush choking someone's loved ones. Druid Ridge does not exist to confirm the stereotype. It is a place whose purpose is to offer peace and tranquility, and the well-groomed landscaping and tree-lined paths are inviting - never forbidding. It is much like a place of refuge – like the quiet of a library, the inspiration of a gallery, or the reflection found in a museum. Druid Ridge is a well-loved member of my neighborhood; an escape or retreat from whatever are the rigors of life at the moment. And it is also somewhere we put our dead.

Magnet

It seemed like the perfect place for EVP – friendly, almost inviting, and I photographed the place year round. So there I was one fall day, taking photos of the turning foliage, my car parked on the side of the path, my tripod at the exact perfect spot to get the exact perfect shot before a storm ensued. I had plans to do some EVP work when I was finished.

I saw this guy in blue overalls walking down one of the paths to my right. It's a large place, but I had a commanding view and I had no idea where he came from. There were no other cars around, and there were no workers anywhere. He was just suddenly there. He carried a long-handled shovel which he held oddly – as if it were a staff. And I watched him almost glide – first to the left, and then up a small hill, as he eventually disappeared behind a couple of mausoleums. I stopped looking when it started to drizzle, and moved my camera gear into the car to wait it out.

EVP sessions for me at the graveyard consisted of shooting a tripod-mounted photo of the headstone, approaching the grave to ask a few very polite questions, then re-shooting the headstone from the exact same spot as before with an infrared filter. I would repeat this process for ten headstones or family plots per session, and then leave.

As the rain stopped, I started my EVP session that day, but when I got to the Harris grave marker, my camera would not function at all. I fussed with it for quite some time – even moving around the grave to see if the physical location had anything to do with the malfunction. I tried everything

I could think of to no avail, but when I moved about 50 feet to another area, my camera began working once again, so I moved. As I was finishing one of the EVP interviews, I noticed that same man walking on the cemetery paths nearby – very slowly, very effortlessly, without much body movement. Same blue overalls and light blue work shirt, same shovel, same thinning white hair. Again, I looked for signs of a work crew or landscapers, but it was just he and I for as far as the eye could see.

I know I'm making a lot of this guy but I guarantee you, there wasn't anything actually suspicious about him – just weirdly circumstantial. He seemed way too old and out of place; too frail to be digging and lifting. He seemed to know where he was going, and he did have that shovel with him, so the best word I can use to characterize the old guy was that he was peculiar.

When I completed my tenth EVP session, I got into the car and returned to the Harris grave once again, and decided to try to take photos, but as before, the camera would not function. No matter how many times I turned if off and on or changed settings, I could not take a photo. But for a third time, I noticed my old man in overalls. He had gotten closer - was probably no more than a hundred feet away. He paid me no attention and simply continued to wander the paths, in and out of the graves as if doing some kind of weird inventory… never looking in my direction; never looking anywhere but straight ahead.

I gave up on the Harris gravesite – I was convinced that

someone or something was interfering with my camera, and decided to return to the front of the cemetery to take some more fall foliage shots. I got into the car and started driving to a precise location at the other side of the cemetery. As I drove away, I noticed the man approaching the huge mausoleum building. I could see his back in my rear view mirror, and he seemed to be floating instead of walking, which when coupled with my problems at the Harris gravesite, started to bother me. I almost turned the car around to follow him, but I was tempted to continue on my quest of the perfect fall shot instead.

I pulled up at a familiar spot, stopped the car and readied my camera for the shot. But there he was again. He had somehow traveled all the way from the other side of the property to where I had just driven in about the same amount of time. This time I was able to notice that he had very white skin and was extremely thin. He wasn't gliding like I thought, but he walked in such an effortless way that his body hardly moved. Even though I was now within 20 feet of him, I couldn't see his feet because the very long overalls scraped on the ground and covered them.

I felt rude staring at him. But as soon as he passed me, I turned around to watch him walk away. I wanted to make sure he wasn't coming up behind me, but already, he was gone. There's nowhere he could have gone. Now I know what a lot of you are thinking right now, and you should; that he ducked behind a tree or a private mausoleum, or something. Anything other than disappearing into thin air, but there was nowhere for him to go – not where we were located.

I've always associated my trouble at the Harris grave with this man. I think both of them are paranormal phenomena, so I sometimes refer to him as Mr. Harris. I don't really know who he was, or if he was a ghost as I am suggesting with this story. But I know he was really there. No short two second brain fart that conjured the image of my father; no dream following anyone down an empty hallway. This time, the person I saw was visible for a very long time. And while I know this runs contrary to many people's ideas about the manifestations and capabilities of spirits, my Mr. Harris was there and then he wasn't.

And if you were to ask me outright whether or not I believe that ghosts can manifest themselves and appear to be as living as you or I, I would probably say it was doubtful. I'm a firm believer in the science and logic of things, and I don't think a spirit can do what Mr. Harris did. He was so realistic that it never dawned on me to take a photo. I was too taken aback by the look of him to strike up a conversation. Ghosts don't just wander aimlessly around graveyards like that do they? Graveyards aren't haunted, are they?

I obviously do not have any answers to these questions, and there really is no proof that this story holds even an ounce of truth. But assuming it is true, and that my veracity is beyond reproach, none of what I saw makes any sense – neither in a normal way or in a paranormal way. And yet, there it was. It's the kind of thing people love to listen to, but never really believe. In broad daylight, a skinny, pasty, old, creepy guy disappears, and I am actually expecting you to believe me?

Now, I went through this entire story for two reasons. First, to introduce my EVP sessions in the cemetery in an interesting way. And second, to challenge the notions so many of us have fixed as fact about spirits. I don't believe ghosts can do what Mr. Harris did, and yet there he was. I suppose I should be writing off the incident as a case of poor observational skills on my part – he didn't disappear; he couldn't have. But I tell you, there is nothing anyone can say to me that will convince me that the disappearing Mr. Harris could have naturally gone from sight that quickly. The surroundings would never have supported such an exit, there was nowhere to hide, and most importantly of all, he traveled every bit as fast as my car and was coming from the opposite direction from where he had just been seen.

I was uneasy when I next returned to the cemetery, and I looked for my strange man, but I have never seen him since – not even at a distance. I tried a couple of months later to photograph the Harris grave, and there were no problems. But I never returned to do another EVP session in that vicinity. Druid Ridge is quite large, and there's room for all of us there.

Out of the 100 graves at which I conducted EVP sessions, approximately 70 percent of the time there was one or more voices recorded. Some were very clear and others were difficult to decipher, but I never considered the responses to be EVP unless I heard a word I could understand. And even then, 70 percent of the time there were results.

Even though I do not believe that cemeteries are haunted, and even though most of the paranormal field would agree, someone was speaking to me at Druid Ridge. But why is it so impossible for a spirit to know that someone is visiting his grave and speaking to him? Why is it not possible for that spirit to return to his grave – perhaps purely out of curiosity – to see who is lamenting his passing? And why is it not possible that finding me there asking questions and taking photos, the spirit in question would desire to politely comment? Even if they had no idea they could be heard, even if they had no idea who I was, even though it's probably the last place on earth they would want to linger, why would it not be possible to get EVP in a graveyard?

Frankly, these are my most controversial EVP. I understand why that is, and as I said, I myself do not believe cemeteries to be haunted, but somehow and for some reason, voices spoke on my recorder there in rather alarming numbers. And I'm not sure exactly what I have learned from that as of yet, except of course to offer the theory that the spirits in question returned for my visits.

But so many of the EVP from my cemetery project make sense and seem directly related to the site being queried. A Mrs. Sappington and her spinster daughter Anna can be heard saying, " Look Annie. It's a man!" Mrs. Roberts repeated the name "Ebony" on two separate occasions as if to call for her own daughter – possibly one of the several

Ebony Roberts in the local phonebook. When asked, some of the residents stated that they liked it where they were buried. One even said, "yes, its nice." When telling another spirit that I would be turning off the recorder and moving along, the voice whispered, "you can let it run."

There are, of course, a great many single word responses – a "yes" or a "no," and sometimes a grunt or a groan. Upon occasion, someone would sound a bit tortured and ask for help. At least once, someone I knew said "Hello, Randy." Mr. Harris and his posse aside, these were people. They said the kinds of things people would say. Very few of them were creepy or unpleasant; there was only one threat made throughout the entire project – the overwhelming majority of these voices were human in every way. They may not have sounded human, but there was humanity in their words – no staccato sounding creepy stuff. I felt as if I had made friends there for the most part, and maybe I did. Maybe each subsequent visit became an event and spirits came from miles around to say hello.

Okay, a little melodrama goes a long way. I understand. But I also understand that my cemetery project felt less threatening than what I had recorded at my own home from time to time. Except for the Harris situation, and the wandering old man, these sessions were fascinating and frankly, a little touching.

I said I wasn't sure what I had learned from this, but one thing I do think is clear to me – there are a lot of spirits around, and I would even go so far as to hazard a guess that there's one for every single person who ever lived. I realize it's not a stretch to believe that everyone has a soul and that, therefore, there have been a lot of souls, but my point is that these spirits are still around in one form or another. The good, the bad, the ugly and the beautiful; young and old – you name it. I think they're all still here if they want to be. I think they're haunting the earth in a strange way – millions upon millions of ghosts haunting us all. Well, I bet that got your attention, didn't it?

They have recently discovered some amazing new things at Stonehenge – how an entire civilization once lived and worshiped there over 4,500 years ago. The rock henge we are all so familiar with was dedicated to the dead – to ancestors, and they would begin each mid-summer solstice there to seek the blessings, wisdom, and care of their departed. Then they would travel almost 3 miles to a second henge made of wood – an exact duplicate of the famous Stonehenge. Here they would celebrate the living, have a magnificent feast and begin the spring in style. The solid rock monument was permanent; honor for the dead was to last forever - chiseled in stone. But life, while a thing worth celebrating to the fullest, was temporary, like the wood used to construct the second henge.

It is no coincidence that we mark our graves with granite and marble whenever possible; that we adorn the markers with flowers. Our treatment of the dead is ritualistic and highly steeped in religious mystery. We have forgotten what our stone-age forebearers could teach us, but something deep inside subconsciously reminds us that we have the same relationship with the dead as the neolithic Britains did on the Wiltshire plains so long ago. It has only been recently that portions of mankind have embraced the sacrilege of discarding and minimizing the impact of our ancestors. We always believed they were with us – guiding or helping us, or simply watching over us. But now, too many of us find such thoughts to be primitive or an indulgence of pagan beliefs. Jesus spoke often of his ancestors and frequently invoked their names and the lessons to be learned from their lives. Much of the Bible is a lineage – homage to those long departed.

We are a different people now over much of the planet, but how many of us can be heard to comment how our deceased loved ones would approve of our actions… or not? At one time or another, don't all of us feel the deceased are with us in spirit? That they're present in our hearts and sometimes in ways more substantial? Millions and millions of deceased loved ones – ancestors, are still an integral part of the human condition; still active in our lives and part of our own spirit. These days, we try to dispense with them – banish them to an afterlife that we see as completely separate from this world – they are gone, never to be seen or heard from again. And only occasionally do we attribute the odd haunting to them, as tortured souls who are bound to this earth in some kind of inter-dimension – a fate they must be freed from to be properly cast out and put away, only to live in memory. And do we really believe such nonsense? Is there a single holy text anywhere that tells us they are to be exiled from our lives? Most scripture tells us nothing at all about such things – we know as much as our antediluvian friends knew 4,500 years ago.

From the moment I recorded my first EVP, I knew something was not as I had been taught. And several thousand disembodied voices later? Yes, I think they're haunting the earth – millions upon millions of them haunting us all. And maybe the word "haunt" needs a softer edge; needs to be exorcized from the demonic associations we've attached to it. Our ancestors, our deceased loved ones, are always with us in ways we do not understand or cannot prove, but they are always with us nevertheless.

By now, I would guess you know how I feel about quite a few things. You've read several chapters that have been laced with the world according to me. I don't recall ever running short on opinions, and I don't think it would come as a shock if I told you that a lot of very knowledgeable people don't agree with much of what you've been reading. Of course, at the end of the day, in the paranormal discipline, that really isn't much of an issue - the field is so wide open, there's room for a lot of different ideas and points of view. But it's extremely important to me that you understand my attitude toward those who disagree with me. We have no choice but to listen and consider alternative points of view. That's it. Short and simple – assorted opinions, theories, and analysis must be welcome.

Most paranormal investigators have their own ideas

about the many things related to the field, and it is healthy to discuss these; to find areas where we agree and identify those areas where we do not. We all see things in our own way and we have to be able to understand that other points of view are of value and will contribute to the work. Even ideas that are proved completely wrong have and will continue to add to the truth simply by being eliminated.

There is such a small body of reliable, undisputable evidence that it is unreasonable to expect tangible and perfect proof from every investigation. I am convinced that paranormal investigators are seriously attempting to find the truth – whatever that might be. They use whatever tools they can find or create to help with discovery, and most of them honor their duty with integrity and an honest analysis of their evidence. And all people have opinions about what's really going on. I don't expect others to accept my conclusions, but I do expect us all to learn from one another. Many of my ideas have been shot down rather effectively and I've needed to rethink and reformulate. We're only human, after all, and we need to accept that no one of us has all the answers.

That said, it is also true that we need to be steadfast in our ideas; we cannot be afraid to take that leap of self-assuredness and confidence, but with humility and a willingness to bend when bending is the smart choice. Never underestimate the value of discovering the flaws in your own thinking and adjusting your mindset based on what you can learn from others.

It's my opinion that one does not delve in the paranormal

– it's not a hobby. It has all the earmarks of one, and like a hobby there's no money in the gig, but the committed investigator would rather be spending time scratching the incredible itch that drives him than anything else. He, or she, wants to learn. They are genuine seekers, and being able to document even the smallest piece of evidence is of paramount importance.

However, for me personally, there is a fundamental question about all of this - one thing that plagues me whenever I turn on a recorder and receive a voice from what we euphemistically refer to as the beyond. Why me? Certainly, there are many experienced journeymen and women throughout the paranormal arena who have logged the hours and made strong attempts to capture EVP. And many of them do, but many do not. So, it's an obvious question for me to ask. Why have I been able to collect so many in such a short time?

Well, first of all, I'm actually not the only one who has done so. There are many people who seem to be able to present us with credible voices. Of course to do that in large quantities is still a very unique occurrence. But it would be, considering that the number of people actually trying to record EVP is quite small. I suppose it is only logical to deduce that the amount of captured EVP would dramatically increase as the number of listeners grow. And that seems quite plausible to me, because it's not rocket science to turn on a recorder, save the file and carefully listen to it later.

It stands to reason then, that there is nothing super

spectacular about the dubious accomplishment of capturing more EVP than the average investigator. There are no handbooks on the how to and what for of EVP, and as luck would have it, this is a ridiculously easy thing to do. There isn't even any investment. Well, some I guess - my device cost less than $100 – way less. I don't employ any special add-ons to improve my recorder's ability to hear from beyond; there are no microphone sensitivity enhancements. I don't even use a remote microphone. There is nothing different about my specific device than any of the other tens of thousands of factory units that have been sold. No special incantations were performed, no potions prescribed, and no unique digitizing elements brought down to earth by aliens. My unit performs like any other.

Lately, I have taken to using my laptop as a recorder. I like the sound quality better, but it's not really very portable. I have also used other recorders – mostly for testing – presumably to see if I still get EVP regardless of the device. I do. And while I like my recorder because it has given me quite a lot of results, I like the better models even more – they're shinier and way cooler. One day, I will upgrade, but I don't think it will effect my results when recording EVP.

I don't believe that my high number of EVP results has very much to do with me at all. I totally believe that EVP appear on my recorder because the entity I am recording wants to be heard. I don't believe there is any way for humans to penetrate the wall between the worlds without either help or insistence by someone or something already residing there. I guess that's fairly final sounding, but I just cannot seem to make it work for me any other way.

I see spirits as being so radically different from us that they probably don't do any single thing the way we do. For instance, maybe they eat – I don't know – but they don't roast a chicken or peel a grape. I just don't see it, and I would love to see scripture or writings of any kind that describe a feast in the spirit world. If they eat, it's a whole other process from what we understand eating to be. That might explain why so many of my EVP seem fixated on food, almost as if it were a long lost memory which they seem to enjoy savoring immensely.

But eating is just a silly way to make a point. Spirits don't run companies and have investments either – not on this plane they don't. They don't drive cars or go to college, or fall down steps, or walk or talk…

They do communicate though, don't they? There are all kinds of stories, articles, books, and encounters that tell us about how well spirits seem to communicate. Somehow, spirits are able to manipulate the electronics or the energy or whatever in my Sony recorder to form words. Might it be some kind of manipulation of the air? Maybe. Vibrations of molecules? Possibly. Frankly, we don't know how they do it, but they do it rather well considering what we hear is accomplished without the benefit of a voice box. It's worth noting that in many ancient writings, angels were seen and heard, but often only telepathically. This idea works for me; seems rather similar, while ironically antithetical, to EVP.

Magnet

The spirit voices we hear when we record come from an entity so unlike us; so alien from our existence experience, that it is amazing we can understand them at all. And yet, here they are – as loud and as understandable as any one of us. That's why I maintain that the recording of these beings has nothing to do with me, and everything to do with their interest in being heard.

When I listen to the playback, I do only a modest amount of enhancement, if any at all. I might try to remove the hiss of background noise if I hear something interesting, and sometimes I will bump up the volume a bit; use the FFT filter. But even these minor enhancements are not needed on most of my EVP, and there's never an attempt to remake an EVP – just ways to understand it better.

So what am I doing that's so special? Do the spirits find me especially good looking? Is my sex appeal so potent that it penetrates beyond the veil? Those who know me would tell you I am average at best in both of those areas, and while my voice is pleasant enough, it's not so full of charisma as to charm any part of either the natural or the supernatural. So then… why?

What is going on that causes disembodied voices to choose my recorder? I've been in situations with others where only my recorder captured EVP, so I suppose it is an easy conclusion to make that for some reason I am being chosen.

For a long time, that thought just didn't seen right to me, and I didn't want to become one of "those" people - the ones who claim to be exclusive and in touch; are sensitive or psychic, or whatever the newest buzz words are. Those people know who they are too – they see and hear things that the rest of us do not, and as a result, we like to make fun of them a bit and sometimes question their sanity.

Of course, I can't do that. How hypocritical to suggest that I record voices from beyond while refusing to accept the possibilities inherent with a sensitive. That would seriously be narrow-minded. But still, I don't experience such things myself, so it's easy to toss a little humor at those who do. Its fairly human to do so – the guy who is different always absorbs the brunt of a certain amount of jokes. It's part of the cost of being different, I guess, but this is really different. A real sensitive is not someone to scoff at.

Of course, there are a bunch of paranormal junkies who want to be sensitive so desperately that whatever they think they can contribute is ultimately useless as evidence. And I suppose, realizing that there are so few methods of actually determining how real one's gift is, these people are able to pull it off. It's a scam, of course. And sometimes it's done to make money, sometimes for fame, but all too often, and maybe more insidiously, it's done "just because" it's cool to be the medium. The medium sees all the ghosts. We want to believe – you know we do, and so we give credence to these people – sometimes, to the detriment of the real sensitive.

As for me, I turn on a recording device. That's all. Sometimes I ask questions, and sometimes I don't. I sense no spirits in the room when I enter. I don't see dead people

– period! I don't hear them either – not without benefit of recording. I am aware of nothing that is talking to me and only me - the voices I hear come from living, breathing, walking and talking, good ole fashioned Grade A Number One people! People you can see and touch, who have families, driving records, active credit cards, and who wear shoes. I don't go into any trances or receive visions; my dreams are stupid, for the most part, and usually only involve me doing something weirdly mundane. I can't bring back the dead, or ferret out a demon that has attached itself to someone else. I can't lead wayward ghosts into the light, or trick them into not haunting a house. I don't even try to make predictions because if I do, less of them will come true than the average person. It seems like a waste of time – better to just be quiet in my case.

But, I still have that nagging question. Why me? Why does it seem that some spirits have decided to talk through my devices? And if they have made some kind of conscious decision to do that, who are they; who were they? They can't all be family members because many of the EVP I've recorded speak of things my family members have never experienced. They can't be simply family members or friends because a great many of them don't seem to like me very much. Some of them don't even seem to be aware I am here. And maybe some of them truly are friends and family, but it is a very safe hypothesis that most of the EVP I have captured are not.

I don't record lots of EVP because I am moral and good,

because, well... I can tell you stories that would negate that assumption. Its not because I am evil and gravitate to the dark side of the force, because I don't. I'm average – I usually accompany my good deeds with a really nasty side of arrogance and self-righteousness – often topped off with some wimpy indecisiveness for dessert. There's just nothing about me that would mark me as a candidate for such a thing.

But there must be something I am overlooking, right? Something that just screams to the underworld that I'm their guy – come on down. Perhaps... Perhaps it just is. You know, like we know snow is cold for a reason, but we never think about it – it just is. Like, why some people love broccoli and others vomit at the sight of it; or why men have so much trouble remembering to put down the seat when they're finished. That's just the way it is. So maybe I get EVP so easily because that's just the way it is.

Do I have to be a mystic or medium, or a sensitive, or whatever that newest terminology is? Because I'm none of those things, and even though I have been told I could probably learn to develop such talents, I have also been told I should learn to talk a little less. And that would be nice, but if I could manage to develop the skills required to help people as a spiritualist, that would be wonderful. Still, I assure you, that if we waited until every last cow on every single farm in the entire Milky Way finally came home, I would still not have developed those talents. God bless the people who have developed them, but I would bet the entire farm and all those cows that most of them would tell you they do what they do just because they do – that's just the way it is.

I prefer this idea that "it just is." I like that explanation a lot. Randy is able to collect EVP through no fault or merit of his own – it just happens that way. No pressure. If I get them, its great. If I don't, that's great too. I don't have to live up to a reputation; no one feels let down if I don't deliver. So far, I tend to get EVP. That's just the way it is. And one day that may change, and that will also be just the way it is

However, I have heard the word magnet thrown around here and there. I like that word. I'm rather fond of the idea of calling myself a magnet – for some reason, the spirit world likes to speak around me and into devices I operate – like iron pyrite to a magnet; a bug to a bug light. I'm comfortable with that, because I don't have to set myself up to succeed or fail. Its not about me anyway. There's no real job title when you're a magnet. It's not something you can put on a shingle or a business card, and it doesn't sound as cool and exotic as psychic, medium, or spiritualist. It sorta makes me one of the guys. Like a position on a football team, or a member of a jury – anything where diversity is required so that individual talents can add to the success of the whole; where the needs of the many outweigh the needs of the one (thank you Spock).

I'll be the magnet.

Truth

You know, eventually we all have to decide whether certain things in life are truth or illusion. Really? Yep. Let's take the case of President Obama's birth certificate, for example. There is ample evidence that he was born a naturalized American citizen and is therefore perfectly qualified to become what, in fact, he is. There is not really any doubt – it is a provable thing. And yet, there are people who don't believe it. To them, this fact is an illusion – some kind of non-truth that, for them, has somehow managed to hide itself in spite of the evidence. This illusion is a false idea – it appears to be one thing when it is actually another, and everyone who does not see it as truth has been deceived. An illusion.

Sometimes, to continue to believe an illusion is stupid – it seems irritatingly silly and is usually a serious waste of everyone's time. No amount of deliberation or heated debate will ever change the genuine facts, no matter how many people you can convince. President Obama will always have been born in the United States, and he will always be the 44th President. It's very cut and dried; a verifiably, air-tight fact. A truth.

With the paranormal, this happens a lot. When evidence is presented, it is often met with disdain and ridicule; the majority of people do not accept the veracity of paranormal evidence. Since the majority view defines the norm by default, the illusion becomes truth, and the truth is labeled as illusion. Kind of hard to explain, but it's quite possible for truth to not necessarily be accepted as such. Getting someone to accept paranormal evidence sometimes seems as futile as building a sand castle with dry sand. It's probably not going to happen.

So, hypothetically – if a photo were to surface that revealed a clear and recognizable full-body apparition, it ought to be front page news, right? I am assuming if you're reading this book, you're probably one of those "whackos" like me who actually believes in this stuff. So, I think all of us can certainly agree that such a photo – of a real apparition – should be on the front page of every news organization in the world. It's proof that there's an afterlife, and that's about as big as it gets, I would think. Experts will look it over, determine it's not a hoax, the image will pass all the most rigorous tests that we know of... Headline: Photo of Actual Apparition. Afterlife a Reality!

Right? Isn't that where such a photo belongs? Or how about one of my EVP voices – "man speaks from the grave – news at 11." Of course, if you tuned in to that eleven o'clock news broadcast, the anchor would be winking a lot and making a bunch of droll comments spiked with references to Halloween or something equally as frivolous. It wouldn't be treated like a real story because, evidence or not, society in general is not willing to accept the paranormal as anything other than some kind of illusion.

I could hazard a guess as to why that is, but it doesn't really matter. Even though the paranormal has been shown to hold answers to many of our most basic human uncertainties, we are determined not to accept it as truth. Truth is such a powerful word – too powerful, perhaps. It's the kind of thing that can crumble entire civilizations – certainly regimes – and truth can actually change the world. How could we have arrived where we are today without the truth that the world was round, for instance – not flat, as everyone at the time assumed. There were people who died confessing that truth; who actually gave their lives and the lives of their entire families in some cases, in defense of an idea that was provably true.

Yes, but there's quite a distinction between the existence of a spirit world and whether or not the earth is flat. But is there really such a difference? At the time, such suggestions were heretical. People weren't even allowed to read about such things, much less create hypotheses and conduct experiments. Trying to prove such a concept was akin to witchcraft, and history is full of people who paid heavily for such actions. Most people have accepted that paranormal research will flourish at home on television reality shows, or as fiction in one form or another, but not as serious science.

Nevertheless, we're not really like that anymore, are we? People don't die for extolling truth anymore, right? Of course they do! It still happens all the time. I don't recall it happening to any paranormal investigators, but deviant ideas are still punished worldwide. We're fortunate in the United States that our government doesn't involve itself officially in such matters, but there are societal sanctions for many paranormal concepts. When the illusionists, or illusionaries, or maybe we should call them illusionarians – people who prefer illusion to the truth – get to squashing the paranormal verity, they thankfully don't deem it worthy of a death sentence. But it wasn't too long ago that they did just that. In Salem, someone's cat died and a witch had to be burned. Make no mistake, Salem is not as the popular lore suggests – it was a societal reaction to an illusion based in fear.

And even though we're all better now, even though the medication seems to be working, there is a side-effect we're still dealing with. All those years of "illusionating" have turned the vast majority of paranormal information into nothing more than the machinations of weirdos and the delusions of creepy bizarro people. "I dunno what weird Bob thinks he saw, but it wasn't Uncle Jim. Uncle Jim is dead. He's such a nut."

My mother never openly embraced the EVP I captured in her house. In fact, after a while she wanted me to stop recording all together – a request I didn't agree to, of course. She heard the voices, and it was hard to tell if she was simply pretending to be amazed or was unable to figure out how or why I was scamming her. She was present when most of them were recorded – could hear her own voice, knew how many people were in the house, and completely recognized that there was another voice she couldn't account for. She heard it with her own ears – without benefit of brainwashing, hypnosis or bad aroma therapy. She never accused me of faking the recordings, but I think she must have thought it because many times she wondered aloud how on earth "could any of this be true." I presented her with evidence that she could herself bear witness to, and yet she never accepted it as truth. It was always some kind of illusion in her mind – confounding and completely mind-boggling, but certainly not the truth. And I say it again - truth is too powerful a word for such things – for some people.

Still, my mother confessed to my sister that there were many strange and completely unexplainable things that happened at the house – things she couldn't tell me for fear I would suggest it was paranormal. I don't know what those things are – she never told me, and since she is almost 91, I don't corner her about such things. But the point is, that even in the face of her own self-admitted paranormal experiences, even having been presented with audio proof, she is unable to accept any of it as true. Well, I like her moxie, and I respect her status as the world's oldest skeptic, but when faced with the facts, shouldn't she have acknowledged the inevitable conclusion?

My wife and I don't tell our ten-year-old daughter about the voices I've recorded at home. She already doesn't like to go to sleep, so why add to the problem, right? But that doesn't alter the evidence, just as my mother's denial doesn't make the proof gathered in her home any less factual. Of course, she is not alone. More than one family member thinks I'm out of my mind. I might not be certifiable, but I'm definitely a bubble or two off plumb. They know me well enough to realize that the EVP aren't fabricated, but they don't accept them as actual. They don't have any idea what the voices are and there "must be a reasonable explanation," but my EVP are certainly not the voices of the dead. No way. No how.

Upon occasion – socially, I will mention what it is I do with my digital recorder, and you can imagine the result. Everyone is initially interested, but almost no one sticks around for long. It makes them uncomfortable rather quickly. Most of the time everyone is very polite and feigns an enthusiastic interest, but it is inconceivable to them that someone such as I could have evidence that essentially blows their entire concept of life and death right out of the water. The subject remains interesting conversation for them until they realize I'm serious and then it immediately heads south. You can watch their eyes dart around the room looking for someone to provide them with a way out of the conversation. They need to get something to drink or eat; they would love to continue this conversation later when they have more time…

Truth

In one instance, a lady was quite enthralled, and wanted to hear the voices for herself. She "believed in all that kind of stuff" and had a couple of fascinating personal experiences to share. But in her analysis of what I played for her, each EVP was something other than a disembodied voice. She was even willing to accept the idea that the voices came from someone else's brainwaves – some kind of cerebral export; thoughts imprinted on the recorder through the pure mental acuity of someone who was present – probably me. A nice way of suggesting the voices were a hoax, but undeniably, none of the EVP were voices from beyond. She was having none of that, and all of a sudden, she stood up and marched away – no longer interested in such poppycock; no longer able to believe in "all that kind of stuff." Being shown evidence, what she had been willing to accept as truth, was no longer acceptable.

And I honestly felt like some kind of heretic; like the heavens were about to open up and swallow me whole, deposit me in hell, remove the memory of me from all of mankind forever… Sometimes, I get the feeling my belief in God comes into question – as if I'm one of those evil twisted people who gets his jollies from dealing with nasty, horrible stuff. You know, one of those people who took Dungeons and Dragons too seriously and has grown up to become some kind of wizard person, who compacts with the devil to gain control over the demons of the lake… or something.

And it truly challenges my sensibilities. There are people who find it more palatable to label me a liar and a charlatan than to even consider my evidence as anything more than an illusion. Some kind of magic - as if I were David Copperfield or Cris Angel, or worse yet, some kind of shameful cheat. They don't even entertain any other explanation. To say that EVP are really disembodied voices is somehow just wrong, and an insult to God and everything we humans hold sacred. And they certainly don't want me hanging around, filling their heads with such shameful heresy, infecting the children, spreading mental disease willy nilly.

Obviously, these days, attitudes are changing somewhat, but historically, that has happened before. Around the turn of the century, spiritualism was all the rage, so it found more acceptance as well as a place in the parlors of the well-to-do, and the avante garde. Likewise, we are currently in a bit of a paranormal renaissance due to the popularity of certain television shows and a contemporary fascination with the so-called psychic arts. In certain quarters, it's not uncommon to have a personal seer on the payroll, and I suppose this should be encouraging to those interested in the field as a serious area of study, but this will all change. All things paranormal are "in" now, but they will once again be "out" and will once again fall back into the depths of anonymity and things forbidden.

It doesn't have to be that way. We could finally embrace paranormal studies as one in a long list of acceptable surveys into the human condition. The fact that quantum physicists are now examining paranormal-like concepts; that particle and wave theories seem to provide some explanation for what we have traditionally referred to as paranormal, is a good thing. I think this kind of exploration will snowball and provide paranormal research the avenue it needs to gain attention as a legitimate foray into the world of science. But in a lot of people's minds, it will take more than serious study and legitimacy for the paranormal to gain respectability.

I don't know why so many of us are frightened by the truth, but it has always been that way. It seems that civilized man makes a point to be afraid of ideas we cannot explain rather than learn to understand them. Of course, eventually some brave souls find a way to seek and ultimately get answers. If there was evidence that could not be denied, we would eventually find our way to the truth, wouldn't we? One can only hope so.

Occasionally, I find it all rather annoying, as you might imagine – probably because I know EVP as a certainty. And if mine are real, then it seems arrogant to think I am the only one. As far as evidence is concerned, as far as the actual believability of what it is I do – the capturing of EVP – I have no doubt and no regret. No fear, or nightmarish anxiety. EVP may not be tangible enough to determine the details of who is speaking, or from where, or how and why. But that they are speaking is genuine, and at the very least, a paranormal truth.

So sure, everyone does need to decide between truth and illusion in life. We need to decide what we believe and where we place our faith; how our faith will add to our lives. Just as we need to separate the truth from the illusion in a subject like global warming, we need to do so with the paranormal. That's why there are investigation teams, and an ever-growing number of university courses about the subject – to label the myths as myths, determine the reliability of the evidence, and form sound, verifiable conclusions.

Truth or illusion… where will we draw the line? Right now, those lines are blurred, as one man's ghost story becomes another's flash point for research. As a society, will we begin to listen to the evidence, discern what is fact, and move into the new millennium as confident and inquisitive beings? Or will we regress once again into fear and the stifling prejudice that challenges truth and covers us so easily in illusion.

But the EVP voices don't care how we choose. I've listened to a lot of recordings and heard a lot of EVP, and I've never once heard a voice that communicated even the slightest portion of angst over whether or not we believe. Frankly, I think they're kind of stunned a little by the idea that we take the time to listen at all. I'm not sure they see the value in it. Here I am, talking about the subject as if it's the most important discovery since nudity, and it wouldn't surprise me one bit to learn that they're just not all that psyched about it.

Most of the EVP I've recorded come in pairs – two voices conversing about any number of subjects, only now and then involving us; almost always totally lacking in urgency of any kind. They're just not all that into it. Occasionally, I think they rather enjoy messing with us, so it's not unusual to hear them take some shots in our direction – often rather harsh jabs at how stupid we seem to be. I don't get a whole lot of voices that give the impression of missing us either. Oh, every so often, one will say my name, or my mom's, in such a way that seems to indicate a wish to be with us. But that's not very frequent.

I realize that a lot of people have a preconceived idea about what is the purpose of an EVP, and that's one of those illusions I've been ranting about. Sometimes, we expect the voices to be needy or anguished; sad and suffering. I don't get very much of that. There's not a lot of Jacob Marley-like voices hell-bent on correcting the errors of our ways, or dragging the chains they forged in life. Once in a while, a voice has told me to stop smoking, or shape up… but nothing specific, and you get a very real sense that it would be possible for them to pass on words of wisdom, but it's just not that important to them.

Among those of us who believe in EVP, I think there is a rather sizeable majority who expect the spirits we record to be lost souls, but I don't get a sense of that either. I would think a lost soul would be dreadfully earnest about his or her fate – too earnest to be concerned with the candy bar I'm eating or taking a moment to whistle. I realize the afterlife could be one happening place, but if you feel lost, you feel lost – carrying on a conversation about a pretty girl takes a back seat.

You see, this whole attitude we have toward the voices is a fantasy. We don't have a clue what's going on wherever they are, or what they could possibly need or want, or whether we can do anything for them or not. But we've been conditioned to think of them as something that is most likely not even close to truth; and if you ask me, I don't know why they would talk to us at all. We spend so much time and effort associating them with negative stuff, I would think we were a real drag to be around.

Take my grandmother – a wonderful woman who definitely qualified as a "giver" when she was alive. I used to call her the best person I ever met. I'm sure that wherever she is, the lady is exactly the same kind of person she was when she was here. She was always a positive aspect of my life, so why would I associate her with anything else. My grandfather was quite stern and very strong-willed, but he was someone everyone loved very much. Why would any of that change just because these folks are dead? These were wonderful people, so if they come back to me in EVP, I expect their voices to reflect their lives. No negativity or depressed moaning; no tormented and sorrowful comments about how terrible it all is. I believe them to be in a good place, and I expect their spirit voices to reflect that as well.

I am always amazed at the sense of humor I've heard in EVP. Sarcastic, silly… sometimes, they outright try to make jokes. They imitate us and do impressions and often poke fun at our folly and foolishness. And they even laugh at their own jokes – more often than not, I might add, as if they've just done 20 minutes at the Apollo on amateur night.

The illusions we often cling to concerning these voices are never very accurate, and always completely assumptive.

It's bad enough that we interpret the meaning of what they say incorrectly, but we always seem to assign attitude and intention. Forget the fact that they are probably manipulating some device just to form words in the first place – a feat that must be hard enough to accomplish, let alone do so expressively. Forget the fact that they sometimes leave out a few words; speak too fast; mispronounce things once in awhile. Earth languages are second languages to them now – give them a break. They figured out a way to talk to us, so shouldn't we just listen and forget attaching our preconceived notions to every syllable?

I think I must be one of those guys who is expecting an EVP to be unique simply because it exists. My interest is not as much tied up with what the voices say as with the unbelievable fact that they say it. And I'm definitely not interested in interpreting their state of being. My assumptions are different. I assume that wherever they are, they've got it well enough in hand and are doing just fine. If it was so terrible where they are, what on earth would cause them to take time away from their predicament of everlasting horror to interject a phrase or two in the middle of my conversations? Why stop what you're doing there in the 9th level of "whatever" to answer my stupid little questions?

I think it's entirely possible that I record so many EVP because I don't make judgments about them. I don't know that for sure, of course, but I think it makes sense. Who wants to talk to some guy who's main concern is "how did you die?" or "I know you had a miserable life, so tell me about it." If I were them, I wouldn't bother with someone like that. It would get old really quick, and I might have to move on, or find something else to do.

So, I think that the voices might just possibly prefer to talk to me because I don't care how they died; don't want to know how miserable their lives were when they were here; don't want to point out that it's "my house now and I don't want you here scaring the kids." I'm just as curious as the next guy, but I don't actually care about the substance of what it is the voices say – not so much. When I tell you that I am a listener, I mean it – I'm there to listen. And if they opt to tell me something really juicy – that's cool. But it's also cool if they don't. Sometimes, just saying hello is enough. And you might say that most of my EVP are boring and painfully normal. You might say that if I provoked them I would get some more ghostly-sounding voices, but I don't really care. It's not about my manipulating a spirit – it's about being there to listen when one speaks. And to give them every freedom I would want for myself; every ounce of respect I expect from them; every consideration a normal person would demand. And maybe that's the right way to go. Maybe they just appreciate being heard for who they truly are – not as stereotypes or creatures, but as the very people they see themselves as being.

EVP are definitely the truth – the boat has long since sailed on whether or not they are real. They are. So I don't understand why we need to surround the voices with our own feeble attempts of limiting narrative. And this is not compassion for the ghost, or sympathy for the devil – it's common sense. If we are ever to understand all we can learn from EVP, then we have no choice but to begin with what we know to be true, and leave the illusion to Hollywood.

I suppose it stands to reason that I would be an advocate of trying to learn as much as we can – there's no purpose in doing this kind of research if it's just for fun. There's not much fun involved in any aspect of it, and when you finally get results, the EVP themselves are not exactly vibrant and dynamic for the most part. So far, they've proven to be terrible conversationalists. Our misconceptions about EVP include the notion that there is a robust ideology or a deeply entrenched philosophy behind the voices. Naturally, I have nothing more than opinions about what is really going on with the voices, but until we are able to get some serious proof, I think it's better to leave all of that alone and just listen.

I don't see the point of probing or filling every EVP session with the sorts of questions that can deliver vast and meaningful answers. Maybe after awhile, we can develop a relationship with one or more of the voices; some way to seamlessly begin to discover more and more facts about their experiences, where they are, and the nature of their situation. Maybe if we took this approach across the board, we'd learn the kinds of things we feel we should. Perhaps instead of hit and run investigations, we should return over and over, deliver ourselves in a consistent and friendly manner, and maybe we would become a part of their life experience as they become a part of ours.

But how can we actually communicate on a truly meaningful level when we bolt into a situation, lay out our best weapons and bolt out in a matter of a few hours. I firmly believe part of the reason I have garnered so many EVP is because I have become a fixture in the places I record. They know me, and they have formed an opinion about me; they trust me, and they understand my attempt is less about putting them on display than it is about learning from them.

And I'm not criticizing how others do the work. I wouldn't begin to tell those with seasoned professionalism how to handle themselves in any situation, but if we're looking for answers to important questions beyond the most basic of "are you there?" I don't think we're going to get them overnight. I think that kind of limited effort adds to the misconceptions we have about EVP and causes a frequent misreading of what we are actually hearing.

What makes me think I could have a conversation with a voice that passes by or comment on what he or she might be saying? I guess anything is possible, but sometimes what they say makes no sense. Sure, I can make it fit into my own reality if I really want to; I can force the voice's words to make sense. I have a lot of voices who say some strange things and my mind instantly struggles to attach it to my own life. It's as if all a spirit voice has to do is be concerned with the minutia of my life. He curses, and I immediately think he is aiming it at me. He asks for help, and I assume he is in pain wherever he is and is reaching out. Surely there are any number of explanations that work just as well.

If an EVP says "I love you" and it sounds like a woman, then it can't be anyone but my aunt, or grandmother. And my imagination can instantly visualize whichever one of those I choose as being lost and wanting to tell me how she felt one last time. She's probably crying, and feels as if her work was not finished on earth – she needed to let me know. The female "I love you" is targeted directly at me.

Is any of that the truth, or have I just opted in to create an illusion? Of course, it's great fun to talk about them and allow our imagination to run amuck, and personally, I think having a good time with this stuff is essential. But we have to know the difference between the truth of it all and the illusion. For all I know, this woman who loves somebody was commenting on a movie, or just plain messing with my head. In order to learn more, we have to add to the evidence, which is why asking questions can be so important. But once again, how sure can we be about a voice's honesty?

It's a very slippery slope, which is why the line between truth and illusion is so difficult to delineate. I think most of us want nothing more than to present evidence that is as complete as it is interesting. Normally, something like Occum's Razor would apply in this kind of situation. Occums' Razor is a principle that simply states, "when you have two competing theories that make exactly the same predictions, the simpler one is the better." But does this apply to events or evidence gathered from and concerning an entirely different world operating under entirely different physics? I don't know, but I'm not sure I want to take the easy road with this subject matter.

I think it applies to how we state our evidence and to the conclusions we draw from the limited amount of evidence we do have available. But while we listen in the field, I think it becomes increasingly clearer with every time out, that this is not a simple situation with simple choices. This is a very difficult conundrum and the solutions might be simple to the inhabitants of that world, but they are infinitely complex and possibly irreconcilable to us.

One morning I awoke with a third of my vision blacked out – as if a curtain had been partially drawn, stopping the light. By the end of the week, I could only see through the outside corner of my eye. Needless to say, I went to the eye doctor, and to make a long story short, spent the next several weeks on my left side trying to recover from retinal surgery. I couldn't even lay on my back except for the few seconds needed to administer eye drops.

Two months earlier, when my heart stopped on the operating table and modern science brought me back, something changed. As far as I was concerned, my life had been saved, and I was deeply happy about it, but when it was dark, as I attempted to sleep, something began to appear on the ceiling of my bedroom. I started noticing spots that seemed to move. They weren't connected to one another and they looked to be moving independently. I had no idea what they were, and at first, I didn't care very much. I chalked it all up to the cataracts I was told would start to become an issue soon. Besides, they were only spots – light areas of different sizes that sort of bounced like jellyfish or squid.

There seemed to be a whole bunch of arms protruding from the spots that were barely visible. It was crazy. Some nights it was rather crowded up there on my ceiling, but regardless of the numbers, they were always there - in the dark. And I wasn't sure if they were the result of cataracts and retinal surgery combined, or some kind of light from the window filtering through the blinds. I did some tests, as best I could for someone confined to his left side 24/7, and nothing seemed to change in the way I saw these blobs. When I was allowed to briefly stand up, they would stay where they were, but would dissipate as I moved closer. Occasionally, they would move toward me, getting larger as they did; smaller when they moved away.

I remembered that two different mediums had insisted I was followed by spirits, so I gave this some renewed consideration, eventually beginning to think of these spots as potentially paranormal; maybe guardian angels or family members. Sometimes the spots were different shades of gray – sometimes almost white. Of course, if you haven't already decided that I was pretty far out there at the time, feel free to say it out loud now, because that's how it felt to me as well. I felt crazy and even mentally disturbed. I even felt haunted.

But the second night after the retinal attachment

surgery, when I was able to open my right eye, the spots had totally changed. I wasn't seeing anything from that eye – just light, which was good enough for me because where there's light, there is vision, unlike before, when there was only that black curtain. Now, they didn't look like spots anymore. Whatever the surgery did to my eye, the spots changed their appearance. The arms, or tentacles, were now very well defined when the right eye was opened; looked more like energy bursts of some kind, faint, neon sea creatures from ten million BC. I can't describe them any better – sea creatures, all floating around the top of my ceiling doing God knows what, watching my every move during every minute I was there. Soon there would be men in little white coats as well, arriving to take me away.

I went back and forth on the issue – whether or not this situation was a result of the detached retina and the still nagging cataracts, or something else. Otherwise, I was seeing things that weren't there. There couldn't be anything floating on my ceiling for God's sake. I mean, come on… you don't want me to tell you that I see spirits and they see me and we talk and they float on my bedroom ceiling at night and they look like…ah…

People have told me that when we flatline and come back, we are not the same person. Could that be what was causing this? It seemed logical to try to communicate with them, but it was all very pathetic. Me, lying on that left side for so long - hip aching, lower back throbbing, neck sore – talking to the ceiling. And I won't lie – there were times when it felt reassuring to regard those spots as angels watching over me. And I did talk to them when we were alone and some nights they seemed to move very close to me – like they were listening, reading my mind. My imagination went wild, because I couldn't get out of bed and often, I couldn't sleep – I had nothing to do but just lie there.

As luck would have it, these were peaceful spots. Once or twice they would get so close to me that I expected them to enter my body as if I was part of some really bad horror movie. In fact, once I stuck my toe right up into the middle of one as it hovered just above me, and I swear, I felt a cold sensation. I was convinced it was a spirit. It freaked me out. I gestured with my hands for them all to stop and I motioned for them to move back. They seemed to do what I wanted. Fabulous - they were good spirits; they were going to give me my space - we could share the room.

As the vision in my right eye improved, the spots seemed to slowly lose some detail. I deduced that in all probability, the detached retina had distorted something that allowed me to see these floating apparitions, and I surmised they must have been ectoplasm. As I continued to progress, I was allowed some time out of the bed and off my side, and I took advantage of the time by trying to photograph these specters. Nothing. No matter what I tried, I just could not manage to photograph a single spot – not even an irregularity in the ceiling paint job. My wife couldn't see the damn things at all, and God bless her, she tried. I even gave her the opportunity to suggest I was losing it; was becoming one of those people who saw ghosts everywhere, but she never took that bait. She just tried to assure me that whatever it was, it was showing itself to me alone.

Eventually, I was released to normal household activities. I was off my side completely, the detached retina was progressing wonderfully and I was starting to see shapes in the affected eye. I grabbed my digital recorder and decided if the spots were watching me, then they would be talking as well, and I desperately wanted to capture those voices – the voices of those fascinating "whatevers" on my ceiling.

I resolved to lay in bed awake, and record for 20 to 30 minutes every night - it seemed like an easy thing to do. Regardless of what time I came to bed, I would start the recorder, settle in and when I got tired, I would stop. And for a couple of nights that's exactly how it worked. Then I fell asleep one night, and recorded for almost 3 hours. Then another night for almost 5 hours, and a third for almost 7 hours, but I recorded at least 20 minutes every night for ten consecutive days.

That's a lot of recordings to listen to, and I suppose you can guess that the majority of what I would hear was snoring, but there were also dozens of voices. All kinds of voices, concerning all sorts of subjects, with a different crew checking in each night. Such an incredible display of randomness and not a single recognizable voice from any previous sessions at the location.

Now before I go on, I need to clear something up. There is one very significant reason why I could not photograph my spots – they weren't there. I know, just when it was getting good, I had to pull the rug out from under this story. There really are spots. I still see them every night, but I still haven't fixed the cataracts. My spots are fainter now, and they tend to move only when I move my head or divert my gaze. As my eyes dart around the room, my spots follow suit. And standing in the dark of the back porch at night, looking over the railing, I can see them on the ground – looking up at me. They are the result of my cataracts – heightened by the detached retina.

And I don't discount the notion that people who flatline sometimes come back with "gifts" and I don't want to give the impression that spirits couldn't be seen by someone. But in my case, they weren't real. And I can't tell you how bittersweet that realization was – I wanted to be able to see them, because eventually I thought we would communicate and I could only think of how much I would learn. And there is the added bonus that at least I know I'm not crazy, and I surely was thinking that a lot of the time. No, my spots are not spirits or ghosts or angels – there's nothing paranormal about them.

But they served me well, these spots, because they started me on the sleep study. I learned that there are EVP going on while I sleep – sometimes in amazing quantity. Sometimes not so many, but the conversations go on all around us as we snore and heavy-breathe our way through each night.

I continued the project by recording five nights in a row in my daughter's room while she slept alone, and then five nights while my wife slept with me out of the room. The only EVP I recorded during those ten nights were when I entered the room to set-up or turn off the recorder.

The voices must be talking for me. They only come to visit me. They hang around wherever I am to be around me. They chatter when I record them, but only when I am present. The damn things are talking so that I can hear them. And it makes my magnet theory all the more credible.

Okay, so who is talking? I don't know names or professions, or any particulars, but during this sleep project, I recorded voices from so many totally different people – saying things that had nothing to do with me. My favorite EVP ever was recorded while I was asleep somewhere between 3 and 4 in the morning. In a slow whispering voice, it very clearly said, "Colt 45 put three of 'em in a hole." How cool is that?! In the middle of the night, in a sleepy suburban neighborhood, while everyone is zonked, that's what I record. Absolutely fabulous, isn't it?

I mean, by now, nothing really surprises me as far as EVP are concerned. I've heard so many different voices and so many different comments, that nothing can bother me any more. "Colt 45..." Holy Toledo! One morning around 5:30 a woman's voice cries out that "Conners is 51 today!" She was so excited, and she wasn't a neighbor or a radio broadcast – she sounded like a robot from a million miles away – all mixed into the static of the night, but so exuberant and so… alive.

My sleep recordings revealed nothing less than a

community of spirit voices. It was like looking behind the coffee can on the shelf and finding the Borrowers standing there, or finding Tinkerbell in the breadbox just waiting for someone to open it up and set her free. It was the craziest thing. Some of these clips are actually very short conversations about my wife and I sleeping. Some continue to call my name. Others just seem to be passing through. One voice told someone to "blow it out his (you know)" while another seemed to be looking for a jackal. Several seem very concerned with how well we are resting, and there are the occasional very serious "heaven and hell" guys who seem to be unhappy. But for the most part, the voices I recorded while we slept were about as predictable as dreams. And even when I sat there awake, staring at my spots on the ceiling, there was an active wealth of EVP all around me.

And I don't know what to make of it all. I definitely feel silly for having spent so much time and energy on spots on the ceiling, and my only solace in that is that they inspired me to make those wonderful sleep recordings. I would love to offer the opinion that the spirits I recorded during these sessions were transient beings who just so happened to stop by along whatever way they were traveling. That's because I don't know what else to say about them, so I really have no idea who they were, or why. Maybe a few knew who I was; maybe a few of them come every night to watch over us, but I think most of them were just attracted to the magnet and stopped by to put their two cents into the fray.

And I would love to suggest that everyone could do

this experiment and record a vast cornucopia of voices while visions of sugar-plums danced through their heads, but I don't think it works the same for everyone. The voices weren't interested in my daughter or my wife – only me.

And I really do apologize for leading you down the path concerning those spots on the ceiling. But you see, those were illusions, and as real as they felt at the time – for weeks, in fact – they were nothing more than a problem with my eyesight. And I've glossed over all the countless tests I did to prove that to myself, but believe me, I still feel a little stupid. There was no truth involved with those spots – they were real, and they were normal. And the illusory disembodied voices, once again, proved to be true.

There is no truth without illusion – no illusion without truth. The two need one another to exist. The illusion of my spots led me to the truth of the voices. Under even the most dense of fogs, certain things pop out from the mist; are accentuated and stand out. For the first time, you notice them as if they were never there before. Only when the fog clears, do they fade back into the camouflage of a detailed and complex view.

Paranormal investigators often have to seek without the benefit of anything concrete to help them notice the unobvious; need to find truth amid the everyday detail of normal life. They need to find the purpose for spots on the wall and recognize the value in it. The pure skeptic would never have heard those sleep voices because he would have recognized my spots for what they were. But personally, I would prefer to merely feel stupid, rather than to have been stupid enough to have missed the truth hiding behind that illusion.

Consequences

I know when they're here. Sometimes. Its just a feeling I get – like there's something in the air, I guess. They don't speak or try to influence me, but I know they are there, and I can't explain how. Now I realize this sounds a lot like something you might hear from a so-called sensitive, and I've already stated in no uncertain terms, several times, that I'm not one of those. I think that perhaps some might suggest where there's smoke, there's fire, but I will reiterate – I'm not claiming to be sensitive. That's not really what I'm talking about anyway. When I say I know when they're here, it's sort of the same as when you just know its gonna snow. Oh sure, the weatherman has already told you to expect "several inches sometime tonight," but even if you didn't know the forecast, you can feel it in the air. It's true! Anyone who lives in a cold climate will agree with that statement – most of the time, you can feel the snow getting ready to fall hours before it actually arrives. There's just something in the air.

That's how it is. There's something in the air when they're

here. If you log in enough hours dealing with something paranormal, I am convinced your body and mind will eventually be able to assimilate it. It's similar to being able to read people you know very well. We've all been there - we can tell when certain people in our lives are going to exhibit certain behaviors – they look a certain way, say certain things; their attitude is slightly different than usual… Others may never be able to pick up on it, but when you're extremely familiar with someone or something, it's actually easy. And it's not clairvoyance or anything supernatural; it's not paranormal and it isn't some hidden gift – you just know. Probably, you know because your mind remembers the conditions surrounding events – especially those you've repeated over and over. We remember. And something in the back of our mind tells us that conditions have changed and something is going to happen.

So, yeah – I know when they are there. I can definitely feel something different. When I walk into the room, there's something that's out of the ordinary, and I've learned to associate that with EVP. I'm not always right, of course, but then again, maybe I am. They might simply decide to be silent. They might just want me to realize they are there.

Fortunately, silence is rare, so I've had lots of chances to associate this "feeling" with productive EVP sessions, and I usually feel confident that there will be voices on recordings I make as a result. Pretty cool, no? I like it, and I tend to rely on it, but I don't expect results based solely on my feelings. The spirits who make the voices are in charge of whether or not they will be heard, and they're in charge of letting me know when they are there.

Knowing they are there brings up another issue. It leads me to believe there are spirits around a lot of the time, so I am also aware of that, and I'm understandably not always in the mood for EVP. I suppose a good investigator would jump at any chance, but I'm not continuously able to sit back and talk to the wall – sometimes I have things to do; sometimes, I don't even want to know they're anywhere near me at all, much less probably right next to me.

And this often happens at the strangest times – when I'm not willing to put my life on hold and become Mr. Investigator. I might be in the shower, or trying to rest after being awake all night, or playing a game with my daughter. If I'm alone when they make me aware of their presence, but have no intention of recording, I opt instead to have a brief conversation with them. I think that's enough in most cases. I'm convinced that's what they really want anyway. That said, suddenly, the conversation you and I have been having has changed a bit.

Well, its true, the conversation is a little different because what I am suggesting is that often there is such a direct desire on the part of a spirit to communicate that they find ways to abruptly insert themselves into our lives. All of our lives, not just mine. That doesn't sound like family members who are just hanging around, does it? Or even transient souls who just want to say "hi" once in awhile. It sounds a tad invasive, but it's not anything like we've come to expect from horror films. I have never run across a spirit that makes the house shake, crashes the expensive stemware to the floor, or turns on all the appliances just to get my attention. Although I wouldn't rule that out too quickly. I have a good friend who played musical appliances with a spirit just recently. The electric fans in his house all came on at once. Nothing else, just the fans. So let me just say that it doesn't have to be, but for the most part, it's very subtle and therefore quite difficult to explain in a way that won't make me seem a bit off my rocker.

Occasionally, I will start to see things out of the corner of my eye. Something moves, and I am distracted long enough to turn my head. What was that? Of course, there's never anything there, and even a quick inspection doesn't offer any indication that what I saw was anything other than my imagination. This happens to all of us from time to time, and just like everyone else, I tend to ignore it at first. In fact, humans are so totally conditioned to things happening on the edge of our peripheral that we dismiss it quite easily - almost always. But then it happens again – maybe several times. At that point, I am interested because this sort of thing may not have occurred for quite awhile, and all of a sudden, it's happening all morning. And the air is ever so slightly different. There is just something about the way it feels. By itself, you wouldn't pay much attention; maybe you'd chalk it up to a change in the humidity or the barometric pressure, but it triggers a memory, and after awhile you are able to figure out what that memory is. You know – they're here.

Consequences

It's simple, really – you do something long enough, it becomes a dynamic part of your subconscious – always there lurking in the background. You're not conscious of it until the trigger is pulled, but it's never just the feel of things; it's more than just noticing movement. Sometimes you sense disapproval. Ooops, my pathology is showing – I suppose approval works just as well, and probably many other emotions too, but for me, it is disapproval. I can be writing an email or working on something totally mind-numbing, and there it is – out of nowhere – disapproval. It's actually quite strong for me, and might even be my most effective attention-getter. I become almost drowned in the impression that what I have just done is not appreciated by... whoever.

This used to happen to me frequently as a child, and I remember the first time very well. I had been playing somewhere I wasn't even supposed to go near – had been there all day, but since I always believed my mother had eyes everywhere, I was definitely apprehensive when I came home from a long summer's day of ten-year-old disobedience. On this particular day, just 6 feet from the back door I was overcome with an incredible sense of evil. Not that there was something oppressing me; it was more like something within me. What a ten-year-old describes as evil turns out to be disapproval as an adult. And of course, I realize how this probably sounds – like guilt. But now that I'm all grown up, these feelings usually occur when there's nothing to feel guilty about; when guilt is the farthest thing from my mind.

As it turns out, there are many events that tell me someone is there. It's never anything concrete – always something very subconscious and very subtle. I might find myself focusing on thoughts about someone deceased – someone I haven't even considered for a very long time, and I can imagine them talking to me. It's a very quick sensation – it leaves almost as soon as it arrives.

There are also those occasions when a series of very small noises will grab my attention. They start as sounds no one would possibly be drawn to, and I used to dismiss them as house noises. Possibly, they're the result of a breeze moving through an open window, or small, precariously balanced objects finally falling. Of course, you know what I'm going to say – after a succession of these small noises, it finally hits me that someone is trying to get my attention, and once I realize that, the noises always seem to stop.

Of course, I've already told you how my doorbell and smoke detector go off without provocation, and that spirit voices have claimed ownership of those events, but maybe you think I'm pushing it a bit with all this stuff.

I would have doubted it myself just a few years ago, but now I actually expect it. I am so completely convinced that this is happening as a sort of paranormal wake-up call, that I don't even give it another thought when it takes place – I just accept it. On those few occasions when I totally ignore the signs, it seems to build slowly, and that feeling I spoke of earlier, that certain something in the air that I couldn't really describe very well, increases until I do something about it.

And the funny thing is, that sometimes, if I still continue to ignore it all and go on about my business, all of a sudden everything stops – abruptly, noticeably, and completely. Maybe they give up?

Now, don't worry about me. I'm not dead set against being examined by a psychiatrist, but that's not what's going on here. What's going on is that someone is reaching out. Someone wants to be noticed; wants to feel a part of someone alive; has something to say, or wants to be in a conversation – even if all he does is listen. And I honestly believe this happens to all of us from time to time. I am convinced it happens to me frequently because they know I will listen.

The past few months I have heard my name whispered, and my clothing has been tugged. Not so subtle, granted, but I made up my mind to ignore those kinds of advances. I don't enjoy having my space violated in that way, and I don't appreciate being frightened or shocked. Hell, I have a heart condition for God's sake. My daughter knows better than to hide around the corner and jump out at me, so I don't respond to these less understated gestures except to say "stop it" out loud.

I have to be in control of this whole paranormal thing. I insist on defining my involvement whenever possible, and I do not take kindly to any attempt to force me into anything. But, sometimes, when I know they're there, I need to be there as well – for them. And it's been my personal experience that almost every single time I turn on the recorder in reaction to one of these feelings, I find a voice of some kind – often only a single "yes" response, but communication all the same.

I think it's critical to mention that this is not all sweetness and light, as the saying goes. Often there are consequences. In theory, the idea of speaking to a wandering spirit may be interesting and might get the ole adrenaline pumping a bit, but after all, this is a ghost we're talking about. What I am essentially suggesting here is that a ghost – a spirit, entity, whatever, has been attempting to get my attention and has succeeded. As a result, I sit down and record a conversation. That's pretty mind-blowing when you isolate it and really ponder the event. It's a significant departure from every day life, that's for damn sure, and it speaks quite well to the weirdness associated with almost anything paranormal.

So I think it is good common sense to realize that there are possibly consequences, and the most obvious of those would be inviting something really bad into your life. How bad is really bad? "Really really really bad." Bad enough to screw up your life and the lives of everyone who loves you to a point of total devastation. Oh, I realize there aren't a lot of wandering demons trying to get into my meager little life, but it is possible. And there are nasty former people out there too, who might just find it entertaining to mess with the living until they just can't stand it anymore.

Personally, I think there's no way to defend against such a thing without a belief in God. There are a lot of people who will tell you otherwise, and frankly, who knows? But for me, it happens to be God's world – all of it; every last interdimensional ceiling tile of it, so I rely on God taking this walk with me. And I'm not a houseboy for the nether world, or a psychological dancing bear for some bad actor from the third level of perdition. As we've discussed before, I don't do errands, cast spells, or conjure anything anytime. I do my best to stay me, and I always retain the option of paying absolutely no attention to anything I hear or see. When I'm certain they are here, I am not impressed; I am not excited or fascinated about the process of communicating. Being in control is where I always want to be.

But there are other, less obvious consequences that come into play. At first, as you know, I thought my voices were family members, and everything was one big happy family reunion. The only thing missing was the food and the flies, but I came to realize that my knowledge was never going to be sufficient enough to ascertain exactly who anyone was or is. I also used to think that that they only came around when I wanted them; that they visited often, but never at inopportune times, and never inappropriately. Wrong! I am now convinced that they're probably somewhere nearby a lot of the time – maybe all the time. And this has nothing to do with my being able to scope them out – it's not like having radar. I become more and more convinced every day that those feelings I mentioned earlier are caused by them; that they can be six inches away without my knowing it until they choose to let me in on the secret.

That's a consequence, and it's significant. Realizing that someone is always kicking around – able to see every aspect of your life goes way beyond disconcerting. It's down right bewildering, and right to the very core. Now that I am aware there are voices all over my sleep, how do you think I feel making love to my wife? Yes, I do that, and I will take this opportunity to brag on my spectacular prowess and infinite knowledge of the subject. But it's just bizarre to think there are others watching me during all the "moments" of my life. Of course, I deal with it by appreciating that they would be there whether I knew it or not, so the only thing that's different is centered around my knowledge of it.

Still, I wonder how many of them crowd into the shower with me, or watch me handle my bodily functions. Do they know when I eat the last cookie or drink from the orange juice carton? What about when I talk out loud to myself? (Which I only do once in a while, so don't get any ideas.) If I can turn on a recorder and get a voice 95 percent of the time, dare I assume that I have privacy during the quiet 5 percent? Or are they still there but pretending not to be? How do I know?

If I lie, they know it. If I curse, they know it. If I look at porn, they're right there with me. If I smoke more than I should… is second-hand smoke an issue for them too? The first time I was touched by something I couldn't explain, it was about 2:00 in the morning. I'd been listening to the previous Sunday's recordings from my mother's house. It was late, my ears were tired of listening through the headphones, and I decided to check my email. One of the emails was an ad from a porn site, and usually I can scope those out and send them right to trash without even a glance. But this one got past me, and I found myself staring face to face with a rather interesting image of a young woman I would not have minded knowing. She invited me to come to her site, and who am I not to oblige a lady – especially one obviously in need of my consideration. I clicked.

Now, I'm not embarrassed by such behavior. I'm a normal man, and I don't have any issues with porn. I don't spend very much time with such things because it's kind of stupid, but once in awhile… Let's say at 2:00 in the morning, when faced with such an image, I was weak. I was only on the home page for a few seconds when without explanation, I was slapped on the face so hard that the headphones cracked and flew completely off my head. I turned immediately expecting to find my wife, but there wasn't anyone there. Now, I have to say, my wife would never do such a thing, but I didn't know who else it could be, so you can imagine how straight-away freaked I became to find no one there. I ran down the steps and determined that everyone in the house was fast asleep and therefore incapable of slapping me.

My headphones were destroyed. The plastic arm was broken in two places – the impact was quite dramatic – but surprisingly, my face didn't hurt at all. There were no red marks, no handprints or pain – nothing! And of course, I have no idea what actually happened. I didn't hear anyone snickering at me from the great beyond, and there wasn't an apparition or a shadow person anywhere on the premises. But someone was there and clocked me good – without a single ounce of pain to show for it.

You know, I don't actually believe such things happen very often, if ever. It goes against what I trust spirits to be capable of doing. It's too much for them to affect such a result, and on top of that, it was actually an attack, and I don't believe a ghost can harm me in that way. I guess it's like that old man in the graveyard, isn't it? I didn't believe he could do what he did, but there he was, and there was I. Slapped like a bad kid making too much noise at the boss's wife's funeral.

I hope the point here hasn't been lost. There are most definitely consequences. There are no free lunches in the paranormal studies program. And I don't even know how accurate I am about the supposition I have that they're everywhere, constantly watching me. I do know I'm not paranoid, and I'm not obsessed with it, but sometimes when I least expect it, I find myself aware that there is a very good chance I am today's E-ticket ride for someone who is no longer living. And that's unsettling to say the least.

But there's something else – a consequence I could never have imagined at the beginning. Sometimes there are cries for help from the voices, and those are the most difficult consequences of all. Someone is hurting. I can hear them. In fact, only I can hear them, and there's nothing I can do. Sometimes they say they're in hell. Sometimes they just want help without a single word about what kind they need or how they expect me to provide it. Sometimes they carry enough doom and gloom with them to keep you up at night

– literally. There are children calling for "Mommy."

I suppose there are those among us who are untouched by such things. Some find it creepy; others even find it amusing. It runs a little deeper for me, because I know there's nothing I can do for them other than to listen. And I don't know who or where they are, and if I could help them, I don't know if I should. Being an empathetic person, you can imagine how heart-breaking it is to know someone is in trouble, in pain, lost, or possibly being punished. We don't know what's really going on with those voices. They could even be lying – just for kicks, or initiating some kind of way to sucker me into involving myself beyond the point at which I should be involved. But they could be in very real trouble as well.

There are times when hearing an EVP can make such an impression that it haunts you for days, as you hear it over and over again, wondering each time what in God's name is really going on. I've been lucky. Clearly 90 percent of the EVP I record fit into categories that are far more light-hearted – fascinating and interesting, not sad and gut-wrenching. But those few voices that touch your heart and engage your soul are more than powerful enough to affect the way you view things – including your own life.

You have to toughen up. You have to understand that all you are is a listener; that whatever is playing out for those seemingly injured voices has nothing to do with you whatsoever, and that you can't and shouldn't be involved or concerned. And that's difficult to do. Yet another consequence, because no longer is it all about talking to dad or Aunt Sue. Sometimes it's all about the stuff of eternal importance; of penalty and retribution; sorrow and ceaseless lament.

There are consequences to this business of eavesdropping on voices from forever. It's not all fun and games, and it's not all ghost stories and haunted houses. The adrenaline rush you might find at Eastern State or the Stanley Hotel is nothing compared to the realization that a small child is wandering, perhaps for all time, looking for her mother.

You have to take paranormal investigation seriously. Of course, there is a time to laugh and a time for practical jokes. There are funny EVP for crying out loud, so there are more than enough memorable "good times" involved throughout the field. But if you're not doing this to learn something, give it up. If you don't carry with you an intention of seeking solid evidence, get a dog and teach it to catch a Frisbee – you'll get a lot more positive reinforcement. If your goals have nothing to do with good, sound, and well-considered exploration, then you're nothing but a thrill seeker, and you probably should do the field a favor and learn how to hang-glide instead.

If there is one thing I have learned, and that list is always growing, it is that even through my comparatively insignificant EVP projects, there is an impact – on me. Hopefully, I've been able to communicate a little bit about that, and maybe someone reading this will realize whether or not they have a purpose in this work. You really do need a purpose. I promise you, there are few things more frustrating than someone who hasn't a clue, doesn't want one, and wouldn't know what to do with it if they got one.

I think at first, most people attempt to capture EVP just out of curiosity. It's easy to do and no one needs to know how stupid you look talking to... well, no one. You don't have to join a paranormal team to press "record," and if you're unsuccessful in your attempt... nothing ventured, nothing gained – put the recorder down, and walk happily into the sunset. But in all probability, if you are able to hear a voice, you're hooked. Make no mistake about it, once you venture down that dark hallway and something speaks to you from the void, you have no choice but to accept it. You've joined an exclusive club.

I've already described my first time, but what I haven't described is how oddly crazy the whole thing seemed for months afterward. It still does sometimes, because I can't shake the undeniably breathtaking seriousness of the whole endeavor. I mean, my God – voices from where? But you still have to start someplace, and those first times are not as easy to deal with as you might think.

After I recorded for a couple of weeks, I started to let my imagination overpower my common sense. Every dark corner of my mother's house became a harbinger of evil spirits. Mind you, all I had was some unexplainable voices on a recorder – nothing else. All the years I lived there as a child; the countless Christmas Eves and family dinners; the times alone in the dark; when the wind was howling and the rain was pounding the windows and the house was creaking and popping – never once did I imagine there were ghosts and evil creatures lurking in the recesses of the hall closet, fixated on sweeping me down to hell or drooling over the great damage they had planned for my helpless soul. Never once did any of that cross my mind, but eight or ten disembodied voices later, and I became one touchy freak. And it was barely manageable because I didn't live there, but when I got my first EVP at home – in my own house...

For some time, I would go from room to room turning on lights. I could no longer walk from the bedroom to the kitchen without seeing every inch of the pathway there. Every EVP I had recorded up to that time was captured during daylight hours, and every one of them was friendly and mildly amusing – bland, even, but there I was – creeping along, expecting something ungodly to leap out and suck the life out of me. Too many movies, no doubt, but I think it was a natural reaction. It's not easy to see the stuff of fiction materialize before your very eyes – or ears. And I decided to keep turning on those lights anyway, until I was somehow able to make sense of it all.

Of course, now I know how stupid I was to worry about the dark, because certainly if something awful was to happen, it could happen just as easily at noon as it could at midnight. Oh hell, I might as well admit it – I was scared, and more than a little overwhelmed by what was going through my head.

Eventually, my attitude changed. I still turn lights on once in awhile – it makes me feel comfortable so I go with it, but I don't have to, and I realize the chances of something leaping out at me are quite extraordinarily slim. Now, I understand that there are incredibly few cases of anyone getting hurt as a direct result of a ghost. Now, I realize that the evil I so quickly anticipated has always been there, and always will be. My direct knowledge of its existence holds no place in the equation. I am no more vulnerable to harm than I ever was, and if anything, I am more prepared because I know more facts.

Before all of this EVP stuff happened to me, even the idea of seeing an apparition was terrifying. I couldn't watch a haunted house film without commenting about how quickly I would move – you wouldn't find me sharing my house with anything like that. Not even Casper gets a spot at my table. Now, of course, I am convinced I share every square inch of my home with unseen entities from near and far – people I never would ever have met in life have wandered in there, thrown a comment or two my way, and politely sauntered off. It may even be that several spirits have decided to move in. Of course, it might be different if the walls bled or the bed levitated but, that aside, I find the notion that I am sharing my home with some kind of paranormal creature(s) to be acceptable. And as long as they behave, as long as there's room for all of us, they're welcome to stay. All I ask is that they keep it down when others are sleeping, and respect the rules of the house – two conditions they have kept religiously.

And that's why I don't believe my house is haunted. It's lived in. The only tangible evidence are the voices, and regardless of what the current wisdom is from the hallowed halls of Paranormal University, those voices will always be completely undetectable to my human senses. I would never have known they were there without recording them. Where is the haunt? I guess it's one of those stubborn positions I take from time to time, and I suspect that the majority of those in the paranormal field will disagree with my stance, but such is life.

Perhaps I take this stance because I fundamentally do not see the paranormal as something disturbingly odd. To me, it's just something we don't understand as yet. Some of it seems to occupy a piece of God's domain; stands with those principles and beliefs that require faith. And the small amount of evidence we do find seems to point to some really strange, but wonderful aspects of life in the greater sense – not to the awful and the dreary. The only reason so much of the paranormal is creepy is because we have made it so. In reality, it is not much different than DNA or atomic structure – it's not easily visible, and the only evidence we have comes from understanding its impact.

I know there is great evil out there, but there is also an even greater good. That's my belief, and I will probably always stick to it. The paranormal holds more potential for improving our worldly experience than it does for destroying it. The paranormal hasn't taken us to the brink of nuclear holocaust. The paranormal doesn't cause a

Category 5 hurricane to terrorize millions of people; doesn't give me bladder cancer or clog my arteries. The paranormal doesn't make me drive too fast or cheat on my taxes; build my house with sub-par lumber or let the air out of my neighbor's tires. The paranormal has never had any kind of meaningful impact in a negative way. Perhaps there have been possessions and harmful haunts that have ravaged lives, but not with the frequency of any number of natural difficulties we all face every day. People often say that we're safer in an airplane than we are in an automobile, but my guess is the paranormal is even less toxic.

Compared to our own scheming, the paranormal has been incredibly uninvolved in human events. You can claim that someone like Hitler was possessed by the devil if you like, but there is far more evidence that he was a twisted dude, whose circumstances gave reason for abysmal and extreme anti-social behavior. Likewise, there is nothing paranormal about SARS or an ICBM rocket. The woes of mankind are directly traceable to man – we know of no instance where the paranormal has interfered with our purposes or our results.

Sometimes, it seems like every bad thing that happens in this world is attributable to demons and devils and all the things that supposedly go bump... I don't know if it's some kind of natural human psychosis to blame the unknown for our own failings or not – it probably is, but not being that kind of person, you would be hard-pressed to convince me that every radically acute piece of behavior can trace its roots to "the devil made me do it." I would love to see the actual evidence that the so-called paranormal has anything to do with the screwed up things man has done throughout history. Maybe I'm naïve, because I just don't believe we can shirk the responsibility we have for our own actions. It's too easy to say that every aspect of life is a battle between good and evil. At the very least, if that is true, then it is within us. Outside forces don't really need to interfere – we do enough messed up things all by ourselves.

So, I consider the paranormal to be a good thing – an untapped area of life with the very real promise of revealing some wisdom about the human experience. I see the paranormal as an uncharted sea worthy of exploration and discovery, not as dark waters certain to swallow us up or send us down the road to ruin. I see it as proof for much of the spiritual suppositions we have lived with since we first arrived on the planet – good and bad. The paranormal seems to hold many of the secrets and mysteries of life; the joy of an afterlife; the exuberance of transcending beyond where we ever dared to dream we could.

During one of those early days I felt a little lost about my place in all of this. I had just recorded my first really negative EVP – a nasty voice that used a racial slur I found almost intolerable. I know it's common sense that a deceased human is probably the same kind of person they were while alive, but this guy was pretty vile and he cursed a lot and his words bothered me. I started to wonder if listening to the voices was somehow wrong, and I felt as though I needed to know what the church had to say about such things.

I picked out a local United Methodist Church and made an appointment with the pastor. On the day of my appointment, I was ushered into the waiting room – a modest room that seemed to double as a library. I paced along the bookshelves reading the titles – it was what one would expect – nothing too interesting, full of catechism variations, histories of Calvanism, and daily devotional type stuff. I think I was convincing myself that this was a bad idea – that I needed wisdom, not finger pointing and accusations. I didn't need some preacher telling me I was going to hell. But it was too late, the door opened and a pleasant looking middle-aged woman came inside. She paused for a few seconds, staring, before she introduced herself. She was the pastor. We shook hands and she led me through a maze of attached offices into an even smaller room somewhere in the middle of the building. She closed the door, invited me to sit and tell her what was on my mind.

Well, I was there, and I didn't even know if I could find my way back through the maze of offices, so I decided to bite the bullet and lay out the entire story – from my first EVP to the nasty cuss who upset me. I won't bore you with all the details, but it turns out that not only did she believe me completely, she said there was somewhere between 13 and 23 spirits traveling with me. Apparently, she took us from room to room so that none of her staff could hear through the walls; said she noticed the spirits the moment she laid eyes on me. "And some of them," she said, "aren't very nice."

I was speechless. Turns out she has always seen spirits – since she was a girl – and she doesn't mention it very often, but she thought I was probably a good risk, considering the nature of my story. I asked her if all clergy knew that the afterlife was different from what we were led to believe in church every Sunday and, to my surprise, she said that many of them did. She said there are two kinds of spiritual people, and that the church is perfect for those whose spiritual life never goes very deep – they expect things to be cut and dried without any mysticism or metaphysics attached. For those people, the clergy preaches, reads from the scripture, visits the sick, and everything else we've come to expect from our priests and ministers. But that other group? Well, she said we are capable of understanding things better than the rest; we see and feel more. She said church services might not be for us.

I picked my jaw off my lap. I have to tell you right away that I don't subscribe to any such nonsense. How on earth can I deal with the notion that some people are more capable of spiritual growth than others? Even if it is true, what do I do with an idea like that? Wander around town feeling all spiritually superior to almost everyone I see? And I like the ideas put forth by the church. I believe in Jesus and Noah and the burning bush... I told her if this paranormal stuff ever gets in the way of any of that, I was done and would never go anywhere near it again. "No need," she said. "I will call you in a day or two and give you the number of some other people you can talk to. People who will understand." And at that, I and my 13 to 23 ghosts (some not so nice) were led back through the maze to begin happily awaiting the call from others just like me.

The call never came. I waited for weeks before I finally called her back. She offered me the name of a spiritualist who would be willing to work with me and help me understand, but it was going to cost me. You can imagine, I never took down the number, and I never went back to that church, and I guess I still don't really know what the church has to say about the paranormal. I'm sure she's a wonderful pastor and a fantastic lady, even if she does seem a bit whacked. After all, she was able to count the spirits following me around – all I can do is record them, so I feel kind of normal by comparison.

I don't believe there are two kinds of people – not any more than I believe there are 13-23 spirits following me around. But I do believe that the church has nothing to say about the subject of EVP or the paranormal, and that's a shame, because truly the juxtaposition between the paranormal and religion seems anything but accidental.

Over the following year, I talked to no less than 4 other clergy – each with a slightly different way of telling me to go away politely. So, I don't know what the official word is on how the paranormal fits into modern religion. I have my own theory on that, and since no one wanted to take the time to defend whatever it is they see as truth, I am sticking to my own beliefs. I'm not willing to change my faith just because I recorded some voices, and I have decided that everything I believe in actually has a place alongside the paranormal. It may be difficult to prove, but for me it works quite nicely. And I think that's important, although I won't waste your time attempting to convert you. It's important because I think religion is the last hurdle the paranormal has to overcome, and we need to finally remove religious restrictions from the way we see the world.

But I wonder... What is it that we owe the voices; the entities, ghosts, spirits – whatever you want to call them? In my case, they come and speak. They telegraph their appearance to make sure I know they are there – they want my attention; they want me to recognize them. I'm not certain they really have all that much to say, just as I'm not sure they actually know how to say it very well. Most of them seem to be restricted to phrases and single syllables – they are definitely creatures of few words. I suppose there isn't time for them to wax poetic and form complex sentences. But they seem to want to be heard.

I can help with that; I can listen, certainly, and I can share what they want to say with anyone who can get online. And while I may be doing it as part of a project, somewhat dispassionately; somewhat void of real involvement, is that where my responsibility stops?

If they're where we will be, don't we owe them something? Respect, attention and consideration – definitely, but is that all? I don't know. It seems to me there must be a reason they seek us out to communicate. What is that reason really?

Consequences

Oh, I know many EVP are residual or amount to nothing more than eavesdropping – there is absolutely no attempt at communicating to us. But so many other voices seem to be genuinely reaching out, so I wonder what is the point of my listening; the point of my being able to hear?

I've concluded that I won't ever know. Of course, it's a fair question to ask – is there a reason it's possible for me to hear these voices? I'm one of those people who believes there really is a purpose for everything – certainly for the important things, and if that's true, then what's the purpose of all of these voices? What can I possibly learn from or do for deceased souls? I can't imagine, but there does seem to be a lot I could learn. But again, to what purpose?

The voices aren't telling me anything. They're not predicting or warning me of anything; they're not offering any descriptions of where they are, and they're not selling any particular religious expression. So far, no voice has had any ax to grind other than personal references, and those don't even happen too frequently. Maybe it's just the distinct personalities of the spirits that come to visit me. Maybe I just get the boring ones because while I find every EVP interesting, I can count on one hand the pieces of wisdom they've doled out. What can I deduce from hearing my name whispered hundreds of times? Well, it's true that I have voices saying things like "we love" or "we know," but there isn't much substance in that either, is there? It confirms something, I suppose – that there are still emotional responses available in the afterlife, but couldn't I have drawn that conclusion based solely on logic and common sense?

I think that perhaps the whole idea of searching for higher meaning through EVP is a fool's errand. It may just be that all we ever actually receive from them is the knowledge that they exist. And that is enough for me, but I still hope for that kick-ass EVP that speaks to the meaning of life, and maybe that's what spurs me on; keeps me motivated, though I'm not convinced I will ever find it. So, is that enough? Is it worth the effort, the consequences, the religious questioning?

What can we possibly learn from studying the migratory pattern of a swallow? What's the point of experimenting with medicines to cure disease? Where's the payoff for all those space shots? I think it's just our nature. We're wired that way. We're inquisitive and interested and we seem to want and need to know. And anything that could possibly be investigated usually is – we find a way and a reason. We're always looking into stuff "just because," and it's not too far removed from the little boy who dismantles his alarm clock – even if he never does manage to put it back together. The very act of decoding it is quite satisfying.

I think we take this human nature with us on our journey through existence. I think the spirits I have recorded are the same way. I think they're inquisitive as well – perhaps to a different degree, but I'm fairly convinced it's similar enough. And I think our need to know is an end to itself, and somehow worth every ounce of the blood, sweat and tears we pour into the endeavor.

I don't know whether you will find this to be as relevant

as I do, but perhaps there is a little wisdom to be gleaned from the voices every now and then. One day, when my doorbell rang and there was no one to be found, I started my recorder as usual and settled in for what I expected to be another series of "yes" answers to another series of typical questions. I felt as though I needed to shake it up a little, so I began inquiring whether or not the voice knew it was dead. I asked if he knew his plight, remembered what happened, and even if he was happy – that sort of thing. There wasn't much response – a single "yeah" affirming knowledge of his death, but all the other questions were seemingly ignored. And then I asked, "Is there anything that you need me to do for you?"

Very simply, in a half-whispered faraway voice, he said, "stay calm." I can attach all sorts of references to those two words – how they apply to life in general, to the questions I was asking – perhaps he was telling me that in the future I would become agitated and put my health in danger. There are all sorts of ways to interpret the meaning of just those two simple words. But for once it was simple and there was indeed wisdom, and therefore, typically, I almost missed it. "Stay calm." Good words and good advice, but the meaning isn't always in the answer – sometimes, it's in the question. How could my staying calm be the answer to something I could do for him? Because that voice had concern for me.

What do we owe them in return?

Evidence

At the very beginning of an EVP session recorded at my home, before I even opened my mouth to ask a question or make a comment, before I even put the recorder down on the table, there was a voice that said. "Set the thing. Sit down." I guess the voice was itching to get started, although what followed wasn't a particularly interesting conversation. Perhaps he was simply wanting to engage in some kind of interaction, or maybe he liked the idea of having a conversation regardless of his own level of involvement. When I heard that EVP so early in the process, I had such hopes for the rest of the session, but you can't predict how these things will go.

The way I usually handle sessions at my home is to record for 5 or 6 minutes, stop the machine and then listen for results. If there is a willingness to interact, or if I capture a series of responses, I will continue for a second 5 minute session – hopefully building on the subjects breached in the previous session. And then, possibly, I'll do it all for a third time.

I thought that if I only appeared interested when I received awareness from them, I might be able to encourage them to become more involved. Occasionally this works – at least that's how it seems to me (you never really know), but most of the time, the voices have their own agenda, and nothing I do or say seems to serve as a catalyst. I don't think the spirits I have dealt with are trying to be contrary or exert any kind of control, but I do think they behave in a manner that's natural for them. I've thought a lot about ways to coerce them into conversing, but I decided to take a page from their playbook. I decided my best tactic is to simply be myself. I figured in the long run, it is better to be as open and honest about my wishes as I can be, and hopefully they will afford me the same deference. And I think, for the most part, that's what usually happens, but they speak when they want and say what they please.

I think as investigators we tend to feel "in charge." We're all big and bad with our IR cameras, digital recorders, DVRs and K2s. Lord knows we sashay around like it's our show. Even when I'm totally alone and it's just me and one little digital recorder, there's preparation and stuff to do, and I sometimes catch myself becoming rather assertive – like it's my project and my EVP experiment, so do what you're told. It never occurs to me that I'm really not the one in charge – the voices have that job cornered. They set the tone. They decide whether to be heard. They make the choice to

Evidence

participate, and without them there's nothing, is there?

It's not like they're all hardcore about it or anything, but it's definitely not going down unless they choose to let it. Truly, if the voices don't speak, I am reduced to nothing more than a crazy man talking to no one and recording it for posterity. Might make for some excellent commitment hearing evidence. No, they're in charge of things based completely on whether or not they play along. It's true that we like to think of ourselves as "hunting" them, but it might be the other way around, and we might be too self-absorbed to know it.

All they have to bring to the party is themselves. Look at the equipment list we might lug into a full-scale investigation. In addition to the cameras, hybrid cameras, recording devices, computers, monitors, battery backups, microphones, measurement devices and meters, we also come packing hundreds of feet of electrical cord, brackets, tripods, cases, and most probably coffee. Yeah. Sure. We're in charge. But it's all good, because sometimes I think it's like a dance. We do our thing and they do theirs – when they feel like it – and unless there's something evil going on, everyone goes away happy for the most part.

I like EVP because the equipment list is so short, but I also like the idea that it's kind of like sitting down for a conversation with someone. Doesn't feel so much as though we're dancing or jockeying for position – just a conversation… Maybe that's why EVP seem to provide so many good results – it's natural. Human beings are serious communicating creatures, so it makes perfect sense to me that a spirit would retain that trait to a certain degree. With EVP, it's pretty much just you and them, and with the right attitude, I think it's "dressed for success."

Once, the morning before a job interview, a voice told me not to forget to wear my new shoes. It said exactly that, and the comments throughout the session, while sparse, seemed completely focused on me. I distinctly felt I was being wished good luck, and that the voice was pulling for me. It's easy to see why I personified that voice to represent my deceased father – the shoe comment was something he would have said. Of course, there's no way I can honestly attach any more to the comment than its face value.

One other day, I turned on the recorder and asked if "there was anything you want to talk about?" The voice responded with a single word – family. So again, I wanted to attach a personality to the response, but by that time, I was well ensconced in my outlook toward such things, and even if the voice had outright stated its name, rank and serial number, I wouldn't have believed it. Conversation – a mindless talk about what shoes to wear and family. Nothing too elaborate; nothing too deep – just simple stuff, similar to what might go on between any two people anywhere. It's just that this conversation didn't place a high premium on whether or not the participants were still alive.

Voices have claimed to be all sorts of people – by name – even a couple of characters from well-known movies. My favorite one was "Jack. Jack Crab." Spoken in the same manner James Bond might have used, this character was from the movie *Little Big Man,* and it was fictional, of course. That was not who I was speaking to. Humorous? Yes, it was a little amusing, and that juxtaposes well with all the other humorous statements I've recorded over the years. I've also recorded voices that gave out other names which held some actual meaning for me, so you can imagine how badly I wanted to believe them.

The funny comments are my favorites, of course. They can be extremely witty, or even corny, and often the sense of humor reminds me of someone specific who has passed, but once again… You know how it is. You'd be the same way. When someone says they want to talk about family, who else could it be other than one's own family? Of course, it might actually be anyone who wants to talk about any family – people I never knew and never will know – that could be the truth of it. But come on! It's my house, my recorder, my questions! But it's not my universe, and it's hard enough for me to get through each day much less be able to translate the goings on of the spiritual realm.

I have to stay disciplined enough not to attach any wishful thinking or bogus intentions that would only tarnish the intrinsic value of the voices. That's really hard to do because human nature demands that we take an active part in the world around us. We're naturally self-centered and each of us often views ourself as the center of the universe, even if only briefly. That keeps us frosty, I think – lets us exhibit the exuberance for life that is so much an inherent part of our beings. If something is about me, I'm guaranteed to become really motivated really quickly; bound to stay involved and focused.

Well, great… so it's natural to put ourselves first and assign identities to every transient voice we hear. Great, but there's no place for it here. There are enough people out there who already think anyone interested in the paranormal is a basket case – possibly even a basket case from hell. I spent a lot of time one night searching the internet for negative opinions on EVP. I actually thought I would find something thoughtful that might help me to either view things differently, or add to my ability to debunk an EVP I was unsure of. No luck. There were plenty of sites that offered instruction for EVP and some that seemed to be skeptical, but there was nothing concrete about that skepticism, and the comments were more scholarly than critical; more centered on method than madness.

But there was plenty of aggressive negativity. I found several sites that seemed devoted to being as discourteous to paranormal subjects as they could possibly be. Name-calling was quite common - a big tool used in their strange character attacks. Religion was another. EVP were voices from Satan and that's all there is to it – unless they could debunk things by using any number of other equally idiotic methods.

It seems that in the face of science, the final debunk amounts to no more than elementary school name-calling or religious mud-slinging. Like so many other things in

America, if there's no real way to prove another's ideas to be wrong, we invoke either Jesus or Satan and the point is won. Saying either of those names results in an instant victory of point because then, no one can continue to argue without being labeled and therefore becoming dismissible.

These people have no belief and no interest in the spirit world because the only spirits they recognize are demons and devils. They pay no attention to angels, or other minions of God, and there is certainly no mention of how Jesus himself became spirit and ascended into heaven as such. No, the spirit world and all its inhabitants are evil, and refusal to believe so means you are either a stupid fool, or a Satan worshipper. End of chapter and verse; from the internet book of Zenskeptic – Portland, Maine.

And here I am worrying about whether or not I allow myself the momentary luxury of thinking I might possibly be listening to my own father's spirit voice. Seems a little like pearls before swine to me with these people, because it's tough enough to try to get something you can call evidence, without having to deal with the issue that your own evil nature rises proportional to the quality of your evidence. And frankly, Zenskeptic couldn't have been more obvious about how he (or she) feels about people like me. Although he never met me, I am an obvious idiot or a lost soul. He probably would wait to tell me to my face before deciding which, but the outcome is already decided.

The sanctity of any evidence I collect in the nature of EVP is at the very least nothing more than a recording of events that actually happened. It's not in my power to interfere with the workings of the device; I can't make the recording reflect what I want it to. That much, I am certain, is not in question. Well, unless I'm truly in league with the devil, which would then afford me all sorts of evil prowess. But returning to sanity, there are ways to determine whether or not a person actually does something to affect the results found on the recording. Therefore, the issue becomes solely what is heard, and if there are voices that do not belong, there are also possible explanations available. When those have been exhausted, what's left is unexplainable; is paranormal, whether Zenskeptic and his Den of Unreasonable Men like it or not.

For me, there is no religious debunk of the unknown – that's off the table. I'm not trying to remove religion from the subject, but we do all sorts of things in this society that run counter to and opposite of legitimate religious tenants – things we don't like to mention – ever. We commit adultery, steal, lie, and even kill – all, a far cry from and much more perverse than presenting paranormal evidence. Yet, when someone presents wrongful evidence in the courts, for example, we never attach Satan as the culprit – something we do all the time with paranormal evidence. Basically, you can lie about killing your wife because you were sleeping with your stepdaughter, and people might shake their heads, but they almost never come to the conclusion that you're in league with Satan. One little EVP offered as evidence of the p-word (paranormal) and you're not only in league with

Evidence

Satan, you run the east coast operation of hell.

Well, for my way of thinking, that's over. Evidence is evidence, and if it doesn't stand up to scrutiny, then it's tainted evidence and shouldn't be considered. But if it passes all the tests then it should be considered factual. And I will happily be the first one to proclaim that I believe in my God and all His truths, but I want it understood that my God does not ask me to close my eyes to the facts of life. He does ask me to have faith – to believe totally and completely in His Word, and that I will do. But belief in the Christian God has never crossed swords with the truths of the universe. There are no scripture or related writings that have ever suggested there are things to believe in that can be proved wrong.

People misinterpret religion to suit their own creative beliefs. There can't be ghosts, therefore, believing in one is in direct defiance of God's certainty, and they will bring forth dozens of scripture passages meant to prove His decree on the subject. But those passages rarely fit the subject very well, and almost never make the point. The simple reality is, the paranormal does not conflict with religion – no more than does biology, geology or any other scientific discipline. Ignorance is not an acceptable bloody pulpit from which to espouse the intentions of the Almighty.

When ignorance attempts to disguise itself as the common man, it is rather quickly revealed as an uneducated void without even rudimentary understanding. Plus, ignorance is not a tenant of God. I can't find a single scripture to suggest we should remain ignorant of life – ignorant of evil, perhaps, but to claim that everything unknown or mysterious is evil is the kind of thinking that has disserved us in the past so often.

So I don't worry about things – EVP is something worth studying to me, and for those who can't think on the subject three-dimensionally, don't worry about it. I have noticed a few atypical avenues for EVP-type communication, which I believe spirits could be using to connect with us. Sometimes, these ideas turn out to be hair-brained and lead to a dead end. There's nothing to learn; no way to offer any proof, but at least, they're stimulating.

One such EVP hybrid is something I call wind talking. I first noticed it at the graveyard, as wind interfered with what was otherwise a very clear recording. On playback, you could hear that constant whoosh sound rushing past the microphone, and since I make no attempt to pre-filter, the noise of it drowned out any possibility of picking up anything but the loudest voices. I didn't realize this was happening until it was too late.

At one particular gravesite, the wind was so prevalent that I knew as soon as I pressed playback that EVP were probably out of the question. I've had this happen before, but in this instance, the sound of the wind varied after I asked a question. As soon as I finished speaking, the rush of air seemed to include a female voice within it. This only occurred after I asked a question, and it only lasted long enough to form what sounded like the syllables of an answer. By the time the session was completed, it gave me

Evidence

the impression that a voice was trying to use the power of the current of air to form words. In fact, it absolutely sounded like words, complete with different syllable groupings, unique sounds, and even inflection. It resonated completely as though forming responses by a voice on the wind. It was so stunning and so realistic that I spent many hours pouring over the file, attempting to use whatever filters I could, to understand the words I was certain were being spoken. And adding to the uniqueness of this EVP, I have never heard it since. I have had many instances of wind on a recorder, but none that sounded like words being formed.

I don't count this as paranormal, however. I can't. I'm too certain that any number of scientific disciplines could account for such a thing, so it is interesting at best. Even if I were able to filter the file in some way so as to pull out the conversation, I think I would have still discounted it, because such file manipulation makes the data too suspect to qualify as evidence. In this case, nothing I did could change the result, and I could not designate it as paranormal even though I am personally thoroughly convinced that it is. There is no evidence to prove anything other than wind contamination of the recording. So even though it sounds exactly like words being spoken, it is better discarded than offered as evidence that could not withstand even the smallest amount of scrutiny.

However, during my sleep study, I noticed something very similar. While my wife and I were asleep, a great deal of heavy breathing and snoring is evident from both of us

– very typical, except on one small section in the middle of the recording. At some time during the night, my wife's snores took on an added dimension. With each exhale, there seemed to be a word spoken by a female. Each time, a different word. Some of them I could easily determine as language – words like "sister" and "I hope to" are easily discernable amid the sound of her sleeping. It was as if a spirit was using her to form those words, to speak entire sentences – one word at a time.

This went on for around 15 minutes, and since there are many distinguishable words among them, I assumed that each similar sound was another syllable or word in the string. I thought this might be another, more esoteric example of the wind talking; using rushing air as a source of power to form language. I have never heard this anomaly before or since that night, and I have listened to hours and hours of us sleeping. It happened only this once.

This is not the natural result of her snoring, and the voice is not even close to the sound of her own. Therefore, is it paranormal? Not at all. I want it to be, because I am convinced that if I could determine what every word actually was, I could reconstruct a few actual sentences – a monologue of some kind. I am additionally psyched because I was actually awake during part of the time while this was going on, and I never heard anything out of the ordinary. The recording reveals that I woke up, and I am well aware of the normal sounds every night in my bedroom.

But as I said, it's not paranormal. Any of the clear EVP

voices definitely are – as paranormal as any EVP would be. But there is no way to ascertain the origin or the method used to make this wind talking, and my concept of using wind or air to form language is nothing more than an interesting theory. The possible phenomenon of wind talking is non-evidentiary so far, and therefore, merely remarkable. I have tried many times to duplicate both of these situations, but I have never been able to capture anything like it – yet. I'm working on it though. But you know, evidence is a crucial commodity, and it must demonstrate or prove something. EVP that cannot withstand the strict demands of evidence are useless.

Another interesting EVP-related episode came in the form of clicks on the recorded file. I noticed the beginning of a series of these clicks – long ones and short ones – that sounded very much like Morse Code. It lasted for around a minute, and seemed incredibly deliberate. Not knowing Morse Code, I looked it up and began to translate the clicks into dots and dashes. Interestingly enough, there were no combinations that defied the parameters of Morse Code – no series of clicks that went beyond 4 dots or 4 dashes, so it seemed to be completely consistent. It was very exciting, and you can imagine how quickly I wanted to interpret the dots and dashes into actual letters. Unfortunately, the letters I came up with spelled nothing – not one single word, and while I surely could have made some mistakes, no matter how many times I tried to translate these clicks into code, it spelled gibberish – time after time.

Perhaps an error could be traced to my lack of expertise. Perhaps an expert in Morse Code would have translated it easily, but my results were so far from any actual words, that I was forced to give it up. It was not paranormal. The clicks only appeared on the recorded file, so it all seemed very much like EVP – minus the actual voice part. But this could never have been viewed as evidence – not by any stretch of anyone's imagination, and all the hours spent trying to decipher the message were wasted.

Well, "wasted" is a strong word, I know. And truly, time spent trying to make sure of one's evidence is never wasted. Even though I need convincing that the wind talking and the Morse Code events are not paranormal in origin, the lack of proof pushes the point – they are nothing beyond fascinating, not qualifying as even the most circumstantial of evidence.

This whole evidence thing can suck the fun out of evaluating one's findings, I guess, but it's extremely critical. If all that is required to guarantee paranormal proof is our own opinion that something is factual, there would be a ton of evidence out there. But none of it would actually prove anything. I have a great many EVP that are clearly disembodied voices, but they are recorded while a television is running in the background. I may know in my heart of hearts that the tv had nothing to do with forming or creating those EVP, but I can't offer them as evidence. That constitutes a contaminated environment, and even though the odds are quite low that this pollution would cause an anomaly capable of muddling the authenticity of a voice, I can't take that chance. It's one thing to call the voice an EVP and to know it is legitimate, but it is quite another to offer it as proof of anything beside the fact that I was working in a contaminated environment. I could never play such a thing for a client and offer it as proof that there are voices in their home.

Then there is the Faraday Box. I personally do not believe a Faraday Box, which removes the possibility of contamination from transmissions while recording, is necessary to record viable and evidence-bearing EVP. In some ways, I think you can make the case that a Faraday Box would prohibit recording anything paranormal in origin. But that doesn't eliminate the practice of attempting to clean the environment; free it from ambient noise, and possible interference from transmissions and appliances that receive and amplify.

Likewise, one needs to know what kinds of ambient sounds will be present at a location. Road sounds, animals and birds, neighbor children, passing cars... There are all sorts of things which can be recorded that will sound other-worldly under certain conditions, and knowing what those are, or being willing to lessen or eliminate them helps secure the authenticity of an EVP. When you are fighting with contamination it becomes quite possible to confuse actual EVP voices with ambient noises. At my mother's house, passing cars can sometimes sound like eerie singing in the background. Also, when completely quiet, her house includes a number of fascinating clicks, bangs, and popping noises. It is my absolute duty to track down and isolate those sounds. I cannot claim them to be paranormal simply because I don't know what they are. In the case of my mother's house, I have been able to discover a number of very small sounds that resonate on the digital recorder as much louder and more purposeful than one's ear would actually observe. They are not EVP sounds – they are naturally occurring, and by discovering their origin, I can now readily recognize them as being just that – natural.

Also, it is best to have as few people as possible present during a session. I used to record a lot of short whistling sounds at one location. Every couple of sessions, there it was – a soft, far away whistle. One of the first things I had to do was to determine who was anywhere near the recorder at the time. Did any of them whistle? Turns out I was the only person ever present who even could whistle, and I knew full well that it wasn't me. But one of my daughters eventually did learn how to whistle. One of the whistling EVP turned out to be her, and I also subsequently noticed her doing it without realizing. Even though she was nowhere near the recorder, this kept me from using any of the whistles recorded while she was present anywhere in the house.

Of course, no one would know, would they? What if I just let it go – it probably wasn't her any of the other times. Probably not, and I definitely had other examples of whistling that were clearly not produced by her or anyone else present, but that's irrelevant. All EVP of that variety were suddenly suspect, and I could not knowingly offer them as evidence of the paranormal – there was a high possibility they could not withstand the scrutiny.

Likewise, someone noticed that before I speak, my inward breath sounds like someone whispering "yeah." Not all the time, but often enough to be noteworthy. Realizing and accepting this made me try to breathe more quietly, but it also placed any EVP of the word "yeah" in question – especially when they occurred right before I spoke. I don't have a choice – these EVP cannot serve as evidence. There are plenty of "yeah" responses that are not the result of anyone's breathing – those can be offered as proof, but the questionable clips cannot. I may not like it, but that's the way it has to be. I don't have any choice in the matter. Evidence has got to be scrutinized thoroughly before it can be proclaimed as real.

Ambient sound can really cause problems. Sometimes, I am aware of background noise that I know will infect the validity of a recorded voice. Sometimes, running water, or the noise caused by heating or cooling systems can become overpowering enough to lessen the quality of an EVP to the point of being inaudible. Sometimes, these devices can make the voices of the living sound different. I make every attempt possible to remove those kinds of roadblocks. It isn't always possible, but if it is, if I can quiet and purify the sound in a room, I will always do so to whatever degree feasible.

At home, I will turn off the fans, televisions, stereos –

anything and everything that could possibly get in the way of creating evidence. They may not really be affecting the quality of a recorded voice, but if I can remove them from play, I will. If something happens while I am recording that might become confusing later, I say so while the tape is running. There's nothing wrong with having a really good EVP that won't quite pass muster. Not every voice could possibly hold up to intense judging and examination. They can be clear as a bell and seem completely authentic, and maybe they are, but if there is any doubt about either the environment or the methodology, it is better to discard those EVP as evidence than it is to force them. Certainly, you have to note that they come from a suspicious background. As I said before, one piece of irrefutable proof is better than dozens of questionable offerings.

Besides, does anyone really want an EVP that's possibly not an EVP? Where's the value in that? I know that my saved voices are probably around 25 percent suspicious. I save them because I am convinced they are real, but I would not offer any of that 25 percent as evidence. I know I have gone to every possible length to eliminate contamination, ambient noise, confused voice assignment... whatever, but sometimes doing what you can is not going to be enough to remove a problem. And it's not about pleasing the skeptics, or the idiots who refuse to accept evidence; it's about pleasing yourself, setting high standards, and knowing that what you offer as proof is indeed just that – unquestionably.

I have been accused from time to time of boasting

about the number of EVP I've recorded, and I count that as a bi-product of making every single one available online for perusal. Anyone in the world is welcome to listen to every single EVP I have captured, and to pass judgment on each and every one of them. But with the weight of my numbers comes the certainty that many of my offerings will be discounted. I expect that, but it doesn't matter. A certain amount of grace has to be granted me because everyone in the world couldn't have been present when the recordings were made; certain situations and environments are known only to me. As a result, I expect suspicion to be cast, but know this – it is not about me.

It is not about how many EVP I have recorded. As I've said before, I am happy to have contributed just one piece of evidence to the cause. There is no value to the numbers – they are what they are – honest attempts at providing my results for others to scrutinize. If I feel there are a thousand legitimate EVP recorded in a single day, then I will lay claim to a thousand EVP. If there is one, I will be just as happy. What is important, and what it is ultimately all about, is to provide some kind of evidence that there are voices. That's all. I do not claim to know who made the voices or where they are when they speak. I do not claim to know what the circumstances were at the time, or what the voice is meant to reflect or what it references. All I know is that I am making an effort to present the evidence so that everyone else can make the determination whether to accept or not. And that's all I can do.

Voices From Forever

Sometimes it seems to me that we are living in a time when anything that might be considered forward thinking is met with a series of abrasive moralistic comments about why we should stick to the old ways. There are a lot of medical procedures which were once commonplace, including infant immunization, that have come under attack. It doesn't seem to matter what the actual evidence is or what studies and research have categorically proven to be true. Certain people have somehow decided that these efforts are wrong and harmful regardless of what the evidence proves. This also applies to anything paranormal for some people, as evidenced by the narrow-minded commentary from my buddy Zenskeptic.

That's all the more reason to make sure that EVP evidence should be as clean as possible. It is far better to exclude even the vast majority of evidence rather than to waste time laboring under the weight of this kind of small-minded thinking. If we provide these people even a single way to correctly question our paranormal evidence, they will surely refuse to accept any of it. There isn't anything we can do about that either, but we can make certain that our efforts are as complete and as exhaustive as possible. We can at least guarantee that our efforts were honest attempts at discovery and not some kind of sensationalistic and loosely-founded forced data.

You know, I have no idea where EVP voices come from. I've offered lots of opinions about that, true, but I could no more prove a single one of those than I could eat a train

Evidence

– there's just no evidence. That aside, theories are good – they're the kind of stuff we need to do just so we can hang a hat on something; so we can begin to view things with a direction and purpose. But if you spend more time looking for ways to bolster your theories than you do observing things as they are, then you'll never find anything. I think it's good to have ideas about how the paranormal might be working, but at the end of the day, how much of it are you really certain about? Probably not very much.

Even the evidence is suspect when you look at it alone. By itself, it's just a piece of video or a recorded voice. Even when you combine pieces of evidence from a common location, all you ever really get is a series of verifiable events – you only get a small glimpse into the true reality. But that's okay, because that's all anyone has at this point. No one has proof of anything beyond these peeks into the darkness. If you capture a clear apparition on video, it can pass all the verification tests you can throw at it, but it's still only a video of something passing in front of your lens. It may qualify as what we call a ghost, but calling it such doesn't say a thing about its origin, habitat, or purpose.

Likewise, if I am all alone in a room with a recorder – no outside contaminants, no receivers, so on and so forth – and if I happen to record an EVP, it's a great piece of evidence, but it's still just a voice on a recorder. You have to have faith, I suppose. Just like religion, you have to honestly believe that the evidence you are seeing is only explainable as something paranormal, and even then, even under the harshest analysis, others might not believe you've captured a voice from beyond. In this day and time, it's too easy to doubt paranormal evidence; it's too uncomfortable for society at large to embrace evidence of things they have always classified as fantasy. We might as well claim to be photographing hobbits – the result would be pretty much the same. Evidence has to be solid.

Hopefully, we're moving into a time when such evidence is accepted for what it is, and is allowed to stand as proof that there is more than meets the eye (or ear) to this world, and that possibly the next world is a fact. That's all we can hope for – to be taken seriously, to have our evidence respected, and to be able to apply it to other acceptable pieces of the paranormal puzzle. The best way for that to happen is to always present well thought-out and deliberately verified evidence. No more questionable items; no more easy to spot wires, camera tricks, or manipulations. That's one reason why I think the value of an EVP goes down with each enhancement. Enhancements feel like tricks, and even people educated in the field sometimes find doubt hidden among those efforts.

But when you're all alone and your thoughts aren't distracted by the sounds and images of a hectic modern world, you have to admit that this evidence you've worked so hard to verify is nothing more than a peek into possibility. And all you are left with are those theories.

I'm sure that at the time of Galileo, there was very little to reinforce his ideas. How could there be? But mankind built on them over the centuries – straight on through Newton and Einstein. And here we are, with scientific equipment and practices that would have been beyond Galileo's imagination all those years ago. It took awhile for those theories to catch on, to attract enough evidence to become fact. Certainly if he had at his disposal even a fraction of what we have at ours, he would have been able to prove his theories without benefit of centuries of development and investigation.

So here we sit – in a golden age of scientific advancement unequaled by any other time in history; where more things have been discovered and learned in this decade alone than in the hundred years before it. We live during the most productive time the planet has ever seen. Possibly in my lifetime, cancer will be cured – certainly during my children's lives. Someone may actually discover a way to fold space in the next several decades, or at least prove it mathematically. Research in eugenics will expand and afford us the luxury of fixing our children's illnesses before they are even born. What kinds of things will we learn in astronomy, or DNA research or, for that matter, in architecture and gardening?

Maybe we'll be smart and invest the money and time it takes to discover what we can about the paranormal. It will have to become important to us first, and there aren't enough of us interested for that to happen just yet.

So, here I am with a handful of EVP – voices from wherever – unable to prove a thing; unable to even come up with a pitch any better than "what you are listening to is real." And I know only other paranormal freaks will care

– others won't even be stimulated. And, mind you, I don't care if they don't care – it's their loss, ya know, but it can be thankless to talk outside the field, and a little insulting from time to time.

What do I do with this handful of EVP? I figure that one day they will be worth something. No, not in terms of money, but some day, mankind will be intrigued, I'm hoping – a great deal. Some guy will claim he has discovered what we already know to be true, and maybe even get his name in the history books. And it would be nice if I were here to see that day, although I don't think that will happen. But, since I was hopefully diligent with my analysis, I will have good solid evidence for people to discover, and maybe I will add to the study that notices the key and opens up the paranormal. Maybe, like Galileo's science, the paranormal will begin to develop and expand; and, good Lord, how many doors will be opened because of it? Maybe someone will be able to actually know where my voices came from, and that ultimate mystery will become common knowledge.

In the meantime, since on occasion these voices talk to us directly, I think I'll be content listening and talking back whenever the opportunity presents itself. It's clear they have something to say, or at the very least, it's definite they want to be heard. So that's what I'll do – listen. I'll do my due diligence and try to provide the best, while least controversial, kind of evidence I can. And all this without losing sight of the ghosts I'm talking to. After the dedication to the paranormal discovery itch has been scratched, after it's all about the field primarily, then it's all about the voices. We are only the last significant part of the puzzle.

But what about the spirit itself? One day, we might discover it's their world too. Might not look the same or even function the same, but they could be sharing it with us just the same. When do we start to think of them as what they are – beings worthy of the same considerations as us? When do we remove them from the annals of fiction and gruesome folklore, and consider them as the intelligent beings they are? Maybe they're more important than the rules of evidence, or the thrill of the quest. Maybe they really are just us.

We don't know that yet. Not really. That's why we label them as everything from ghouls to demons; that's why they are ectoplasm and rods to us – because we don't know who they are yet. But one day we will, you know. One day one of these pieces of evidence will lead some stray investigator or scientist into the right place with the right concepts to discover that one tiny smidgen of evidence that gives us all entry into the ultimate truth. But for now – we don't really know.

And the odds are these voices I talk about are many things, and I have a feeling that, for me, I will know one day soon whether or not I will be joining them. The odds are I will. All the non-evidence points to it. All the deeply buried knowledge, the feelings and inklings, the self-preservation inherent within our species, and the idea that we were made in our creator's image, all point to the likelihood that what we sense is more provable in the long run than the evidence we are able to accumulate today.

I'm willing to bank on it being so. I think I am not alone either, because deep down inside, for some unexplainable reason, we all realize where we're headed. And it's fully fitting that we don't know for sure, because nothing worth having comes without first having the faith that it's worth the wait. And these voices? I can't prove it. No one can – not yet, but it probably is us – transcendent and transformed – but us just the same.

Hope

What does it all mean? That's a fair question, and I would love to be able to pontificate lucidly enough to tell you what it all means. But I can't. I talk a lot – it's a long suit of mine, but I'm short on answers to a question as big as that. What does it all mean? I ask myself that question at least once a week, because it's incredibly important, but I just can't seem to come up with a permanent answer. I have all sorts of quick little reactions that fit a given individual moment, but they're like Hershey Kisses – they taste great, but one just isn't enough.

Each EVP is like a Hershey Kiss as well, and likewise, one is never enough either. That's such a superficial way to describe something as meaningful as a voice from beyond. I mean, think about the immense significance of such an event. A voice from beyond good Lord, that's wicked heavy! We are actually able to hear speech from someone not of this world, and sometimes, the voice is speaking directly to us – as individuals. Not just to all of mankind, because that would be amazing enough to hear a voice from beyond with a message for all mankind. You might even expect something like that in a strange way, but no! It's a voice speaking to me, for instance, concerning itself with my little life and my insignificant problems, answering what amount to inane questions posed by me – all from an entity who heralds from God knows where.

So, I ask again, what does it all mean? There must be a purpose; some kind of eventual necessity, perhaps; maybe some indication that salvation is nigh. Are these voices actually ghosts? Mankind has been talking about ghosts and spirits since the beginning. As children, we lie awake at night worried about what's under the bed or in the closet. We drive our parents crazy with the rituals and defense mechanisms we go through each night as we literally wait for an evil menace to figure out a way to beat our defenses and "get us." God knows what these monsters are supposed to do to us once they "get us," but it surely must be their main goal – the meaning of their existence. And no amount of common sense is salvo enough to rid us of this irrational fear and trepidation.

As adults, we lie awake at night... well, staring at spots on the ceiling, perhaps, and wondering whether or not the spirits inside those spots are going to sneak inside our bodies as we sleep. Everyone knows a spirit's main purpose in life is to get inside of our miserably limited bodies and do what we do every day. We never even give it a thought that the odds are very high – incredibly high – that there's nothing so envious about our bodies to cause spirits worldwide to line up, just dying (again) to get their hands on us. And, in spite of this craving to inhabit humans and possess us, they wait patiently on my ceiling until I fall asleep before they pounce. As if they couldn't just do it whenever the urge hit them.

I guess what I'm trying to say is that we're weird. We hide from the strangest things; fear things we know nothing about; build wild untruths about stuff and then spend the rest of our lives being afraid of the very stuff we invent. We're just so damn peculiar.

Personally, I think it's time we all grew up, don't you? Time we dispensed with the fears we know to be unfounded and embrace the unknown with caution, but with passion and a sense of enlightenment. Think of all the things mankind has learned that were born out of fear. I think the time has come to dispense with it. Let's continue to be afraid of erratic drivers and little kids with matches, or too much cholesterol on top of a grease diet, global warming and changes in the earth's magnetic field. But no more with the creatures under the bed, or the possibility that grandma might still be living in the house 20 years after her death.

My mother and I were talking about visiting her childhood home in Scranton once again before she passes away. I spent many a summer there myself; made friends – it was my second home. My father's grave is there, mom's brother still lives nearby, and she wonders what happened to the house. My mother grew up in that house – passed through all the important moments in her young life there, and it was a central point for all of us in the family as we spread out over the years. It was a kind of zero point field for everyone as we would return for holidays, and sometimes just because.

It was almost a hallowed place for me – the wide wooden stairs, the ancient grandfather clock chiming its way through time every fifteen minutes; the stained glass windows in the dining room; the old-fashioned wallpaper and 1930s electrical switches. I took my first steps there one Easter visit; played whiffle ball down the block; rocked on the front porch every Sunday morning watching passersby all dressed up in their Sunday finest. The street hucksters in the early summer mornings sometimes slowed me awake with their calls. "Huckleberries. Fresh-picked huckleberries." Sometimes I would lean out the upstairs bedroom window and mimic them as they passed by, and they would feign anger, shake their fists mockingly in return, but always with smiles and laughter. My grandmother and I would walk to "the corners" – to the butcher shop and the bakery, to Cosgrove's store and the bank. We'd stop by Mrs. Mike's for a chat, and she would give me chocolates from a box or red licorice or sometimes, a nickel.

I remember Uncle Nick – occasionally kicked out by Aunt Mary for too much drinking or whenever her "insanity" was acting up. Beebee and Charlie – the world's nicest people; Lillian and Ed; Aunt Helen and Uncle Bill; Elaine, Hilda and Frank. They're all gone now - every last

Hope

one of them, except for my mother and uncle. After my Aunt Dorothy passed away, they sold the house, and now someone else has the pleasure of building memories and growing their lives within its walls.

I recently told my mother that if she really wanted to know what had happened to the old place, we should just go and knock on the door. Ask the new owners for one last look at more than a century of family memories - my mother's lost youth; walls that absorbed the seconds of her life and soaked up the excess tears and laughter. I suggested we could explain it to them. She was in her nineties, and needed so little from life now – just one last look. Surely they would let us in.

When I heard this conversation on my recorder, it included a third voice – a thick, male voice – direct and deliberate; someone who wasn't actually there. Well, not so you could prove it anyway. "Don't do it," the voice said. "No."

I'm not sure how much credence one should give to such a comment from such a voice. Based on almost every opinion I've promoted right here in this book, I cannot assume this voice to be anyone specific, and the words could reference anything. There is no guarantee that those words were even meant for us, were even part of our conversation. But you listen to such things when you hear them. When a voice speaks from "that place," you pay attention, and at the very least, it was good advice, even if it could have been accidental. It spoke wisely – gave us truth.

We expect so much instant gratification in this society, so maybe the paranormal isn't instantly rewarding enough, or revealing enough, or even spectacular enough. Maybe we're not satisfied just listening in on whatever the voices have to say unless it;s immediately recognizable as prophetic or wise. Maybe 95 percent of the EVP I've recorded are just too day-to-day for most of us, with no impact on our daily lives, no secrets to the universe – not even a glance into the afterlife. What good are they if they hold no bearing on the stuff of life, or scare us into acceptance?

We know they're real though. We can claim they're something else if that makes us feel better, because it's alright to rationalize our way through truth – we're good at it. Always have been. So, it really doesn't matter if we want to stare evidence in the face and call it hocus pocus or wishful thinking. But that defeats the purpose of looking in the first place, doesn't it? I don't know about you, but when I go looking for something, I rejoice when I find it. There's a sense of accomplishment – especially when I set out on a quest to find it. So you won't see me searching for the paranormal only to disavow the evidence when it hits me in the face.

No, there's no amount of irrational reordering of my brain cells that will cause me to abandon the results of this quest. I hear them, these voices, and if you've read this far, you probably agree they're real. So, if we're going to grow up and face the world with eyes wide open, EVP is a great place to start.

These voices can only be one of two things, you know. An honest-to-God EVP might be the voice of deceased humans, and all the junk we've been led to believe about ghosts just might be true. Or, EVP could also be non-human spirits – demons, angels, aliens, fairies, whatever… EVP come from somewhere, and as far as I can tell, it's got to be one or the other. Well, of course, there is a third possibility – it could be both of them. The voices we record could come from anyone of the billions of earth's deceased – everyone who ever walked the planet still holds a lifetime pass to all the rides, concessions and side shows. And the non-humans? Well, it's their job, isn't it?

We know the voices are real! We should stop pretending to the contrary. It should bother us all to hear someone trash the whole process and carelessly toss out the results, because we know what's up, don't we? Let's be totally honest with one another. With a show of hands, who believes that EVP are a paranormal reality? (I see one or two hold-outs, and it figures – there's always someone who doesn't pay attention to the facts.)

There are voices out there talking, and for some inexplicable reason, we have been able to record them. How absolutely bizarre! But true. So, enough with the hyperbole and the descriptive words – repeat after me… "I do believe I do believe I do I do I do believe." I am as convinced about the reality of my EVP voices as I am that I love my children. It doesn't take a terribly great constitution to admit to that, does it?

EVP are universal within the field. They have been captured all over the earth, by all manner of investigators, on all sorts of different digital recorders, video cameras and actual reel to reels. They constitute the most prolific body of evidence within the field. Where there's a paranormal investigator, there's a recording device, and from my experience, there are EVP.

And if you're complacently sitting there and you still have your doubts, then I guess you should be very careful you don't just wander off the earth and fall into space when you reach the edge. Don't even bother to fill that prescription for antibiotics – surely a pill won't stop the infection. If God had wanted us to fly, he'd have given us wings. The voices on my recordings, and the recordings of countless other individuals couldn't be real – there must be some other explanation. And I wonder how many generations will pass before we finally start to laugh at our ignorance and our informed inability to believe our own senses.

Well, you can languish in the bliss of ignorance if you like, but the rest of us are moving forward. We know the voices are true, but there is so much we don't know, and it's time to get to steppin'. Who are they? Where do they come from? What is the purpose? How do they communicate? What is it like where they are? What do they retain from this world? On and on the questions go – so many mysteries still out there to solve, so let's get on with it. Let's stop kidding ourselves, and start finding some new solutions. Lord knows we've rotted and decayed long enough. Put the crayons down and sharpen our pencils, coloring within the lines is no longer possible. It's a different world than we thought.

My latest project is aimed at trying to identify a voice – just one. I don't care which one, but I thought it would be a good idea to start at the beginning, and for me, that means my father. I've started asking for him by name. I've asked whoever might be listening to put out the word that Randy Keller was trying to reach his dad. I started talking to him personally a lot, sharing my feelings about our lives together; discussing my disappointments and joys. I am trying to get just one indication that he specifically is listening, and be able to find a way to know if he speaks.

It makes sense to me to start with him, for truly it was his passing that brought me here in the first place. Had it not taken me so long to grieve, I might never have tried at all, but all things work out for the best if you choose to view them so, and my need to communicate with him was my catalyst. It's only fitting I should go in his direction.

So far, not much luck. There are voices on my recordings, but none of them have indicated that it's him – not yet. But there was this one response that has me thinking I just might succeed. How great will that be when the day comes I can determine who is actually speaking. The response didn't come as an answer to any of my questions; wasn't a comment on my behavior or any of the words I spoke, or emotions I tried to express. Quite simply, the voice said, "Is that Randy?" – quietly, but very clearly – as if the speaker really wasn't certain, as if they heard my pleas and my angst

– maybe out of what constitutes nowhere to them – and it dawned on them that it sounded a lot like it could be me?

I mean, I'm probably wrong here, but for just a second, think about it. Maybe they're as lost in this process as we are? Maybe there are ways they can hear us, see us, find us, recognize us, but they're not completely sure either. Maybe they have moments of clarity surrounded by confusion and disorientation. Maybe everything is just fine where they are, but when they get involved with us, it all gets a little muddy. Maybe maybe maybe. I don't know what it means, but I know there is something new to focus on. There is something to shoot for – a new pursuit. As far as I'm concerned, a lot of us have probably begun to move beyond the labor of proving the voices truly exist, and recognize that it's time to learn more.

And I don't know what "is that Randy?" means. Not yet. But it tells me something is consciously involved. I need to think it out, ask better questions – the right questions. I know the mediums and psychics already have it all figured – they know who is who on the other side, but we only have their word for it, and that's not acceptable evidence. I don't fit into their league, and neither do most of you, so we need to find another way. Maybe it won't be me that discovers this answer at all – maybe it will be someone else. You, for instance. There are enough questions, and since we know EVP hold some answers, there's something concrete to work with. Maybe some of us will focus on where they live. Others might be more interested in discovering how they

Hope

let us hear them. I already told you what I'm working on – a way to identify them. Maybe we'll pool our resources and share information.

Wait. That's not going to happen, is it? We won't pool anything. Paranormal people don't play well together, and they don't share, do they? How many times have we drooled over someone else's evidence, secretly wishing it were ours, and then verbally trash it to whomever will listen? How many blog entries have I read from investigators who mercilessly criticize their fellow travelers' evidence. In my own case, did it really take two years before anyone in the field bothered to answer an email or recognize a single EVP I'd recorded? Yes. It did take two years, and I don't know why, but I do know it wasn't just a bad time for everyone in the field, and it also wasn't very supportive. We should all be supporting one another through thick and thin. We should be finding constructive ways to critique evidence others present, and readily accept good evidence at its face value.

If Bob in Montana has just captured what he thinks is an apparition on video, shouldn't he be able to call Hank in North Carolina for some outside analysis? It would be nice to have help explaining the possible photographic origins of that translucent, vapor-like woman's figure standing in the corner of the photo. Shouldn't he be able to ask Hank for his opinion without having to endure Hank's resentment issues? Shouldn't there be hundreds, if not thousands, of others throughout the country that could offer some help in debunking or proving the photo? How about throughout the entire world?

Maybe Bjorn in Sweden gets very good results with some special technique he uses. Bjorn is ready and willing to tell every last one of us how it's done, right? We can use that information on our own investigations, and if it works, then we'll let others know all about it. Who knows? Maybe someone will improve on the process. Maybe one day, we'll take photos of apparitions all the time because of what we learned from Bjorn. And maybe there are rats on the moon. Maybe Jessica Rabbit is not a cartoon.

The paranormal bunch is too covetous and selfish for any of that to happen. On the local level, it's every man for himself, and I frankly don't understand it. If our techniques are so fabulous, then why don't we have more results than we do? We can all stand to pick up some tips. Can't we learn from the rest of us? I know I could certainly learn from every single serious investigator that grabs a flashlight and climbs into a crawlspace or attic on a rainy night. Every resolute investigation that occurs might hold some important information that could further the field of study tremendously. But we won't be doing that, will we? Some of us might, but not most of us.

We'll say we will, but it'll never happen. One group will feel superior because they have a long history and lots of results. Another group will be quick-tempered and moody because they're new and have nothing to show. The new group will dislike the successful one. There won't be a good reason, but they'll find something. And the successful

Hope

well-established team won't want to take suggestions from someone like me, even if I just might have something they can use to ease the fear and utter hopelessness of a terrified client.

We have to share information and ideas. We need to review one another's results and conclusions, we need to be able to find one another quickly and ask questions; we need to answer those questions. I've placed every single bona fide EVP I have ever recorded online. Anyone in the entire world who can get online will have instant access to the entire bunch. I put descriptions of the surroundings at the time of the recording, explain what I can about the whereabouts of everyone present at the time, and include session notes as an attempt to share what I think I've learned. I want to share every single piece of EVP evidence I have ever gathered. And on top of that, if I get any other evidence – a photo or a video, even an experience – I will put that online as well.

I do all of this thinking I will be contributing to a field of study; to a scholarly endeavor where every-day blokes like myself might be leading the vanguard of investigation and research into the most "out there" and exciting area of study of all time. I thought others would be interested and applaud me for the organizational aspects of my evidence. I thought they would be thrilled to have my proof as a mini-library; maybe they would hear something that would aid them in their own research, and they would tell me it was helpful; I would feel encouraged to carry on knowing my work was of benefit.

I honestly thought all of that, and a whole lot more. I was as naïve as a small child with a stack of Playboys under his bed. I didn't know what to do with them all, but I knew they were worth something to somebody. Apparently not.

And it's such a shame and a waste of resources. We should be compiling volumes about what we know and what we're certain is not accurate; about the myriad of methodologies that work in a myriad of situations; information about equipment – the properties of different manufacturers and what kind of results to expect. Does anyone know if heavy condensation can contribute to the increase or lack of EVP on a recorder from a certain company? Are FLIR devices likely to work better in warm climates? What's really happening with that whole battery drain thing?

We should be collating all our evidence – registering it in such a way that others can refer to it when and if they need. Perhaps what I discover about a poltergeist in Maryland will shed some light on a case in California. Maybe we'll be able to put to rest the controversy concerning the origin of poltergeist. Maybe we'll be able to look up what a hundred other investigations have to say or show about the exact same thing our client is suffering with right now.

We should be comparing EVP voices. We should be plotting graphs based on the time of day EVP have been recorded. Maybe they speak more after midnight; maybe they are more active early in the morning. We should universally adhere to strict guidelines for what defines an A-classification as opposed to a D. Are there ways to use

Hope

imaging equipment in conjunction with EVP to form a picture of what or who is speaking? Has anyone figured out a method to discover where the voice emanates from?

Is any of this ever going to be possible? We all know the answer is probably "no." So, why not? Are we really so perversely envious of one another that we can't manage to share? What if your equipment breaks? Maybe a neighboring team can help you out. Or maybe you can borrow a couple of members to help you properly cover that big mental hospital. It should be that way, no?

We don't need blog entries telling us about how Team A is right about stuff but Team B is full of idiots and posers. We don't need books that claim to know everything there is to know about the proper investigative techniques – we need books that offer us different possibilities. We need websites that share information, and put us in touch with all the rest of us. We need to talk to one another respectfully, and be willing to learn; be just as willing to teach.

When I talk to people in the field, I get all sorts of reasons why none of this will ever come to pass, and frankly, its rubs me raw. If we cannot work together for the common good; cannot pool resources and share ideas; cannot encourage, support and help our fellow seekers, then we need to get out of the way and stop retarding the very thing we want so badly to advance.

You know, there are only two ways to learn anything – either through experience, or by being told. I have learned a lot through both of these paths, and I am completely convinced that I need to be open to both. I expect there will be people who find the things I have said in this book to be as wrong as wrong can be. I expect that, and I would be amazed if it didn't play out exactly that way. I also expect there will be others who find what I've said to be informative and useful. There might even be one or two nuts out there who think I'm the smartest guy in the whole world; probably more who think I'm an idiot. But from whom am I going to learn more – those who agree with my every word or those who don't? The answer to that question should be obvious. I need to hear it all if I'm going to grow in the field; in any field, for that matter – this is as necessary in medicine as it is in architecture.

I'm certain as certain can be that if you check back with me somewhere down the road, there will be things I've changed my mind about. Someone will have schooled me on a few issues – maybe even given me great cause to rethink every bit of it. That's how it is with the paranormal – you know less than you think and more than you realize, and nothing is ever a slam dunk. We owe each other more than the jealous indifference we exhibit so readily, and the quiet belligerence we offer when asked for our help.

I've heard that part of the problem is that there are so many newcomers to the field. It's not the actual numbers, but what's behind them. So many so-called paranormal investigators are nothing more than people who think it's cool to walk around in the dark carrying a flashlight and insulting dead people. That makes it tough on the newcomers that are serious – people like me, I guess.

So much of what gives someone credibility is their behavior. Maybe that's unfortunate, because there must be a number of investigators out there with the personality of Mussolini, but with mad skills. So, I wonder what it is that prevents people from doing this aspect of their jobs right. I've heard so many amazing stories about bad behavior – everything and anything you can think of, but in the last several months, it's really been bothering me.

We've got to get our act together, and this goes beyond any pleas for unity. We've simply got to behave ourselves. And I'm not going to list the things we're doing wrong because I really don't want to end on such a note, but we all know what I'm talking about. It shouldn't take someone like me to point out the value of being polite, but the horror stories of rude investigators disrespecting clients and property (not to mention one another) is a real shocker for this newbie. My mother taught me better than that. Why on earth would anyone think they can go into someone else's home and behave like spoiled demon seed – especially when they're supposed to be solving a dangerous and frightening problem. All we do is add to a client's grief when we display bad-ass behavior.

There are locations around my city that refuse to allow paranormal teams access because of the conduct of those who preceded. Fence-hopping is not unheard of, and utter disregard for the grounds and buildings through littering, is unacceptable. Broken items in people's houses is deplorable.

And it's probably only a few individuals who manage to make the rounds, but when you couple this behavior with an appalling and self-important attitude, it's no wonder eyes roll and heads shake when a team asks for permission, or tries to help. A woman I met once told me it was worse having them in her house than dealing with the problems she was experiencing.

The rotten behavior comes from badly-run groups and teams, with a lack of leadership and a minimal interest in the paranormal. It cannot continue. Team leaders have to get their acts together and educate members or be more selective with who joins. There should be purposeful and consistent meetings, rules of engagement, and the understanding that what one individual does shines even brighter on the entire group.

I know a founder who has removed members for a single infraction. Not because he's a tough S.O.B., but because allowing the individual to continue would destroy his team's reputation. Founders and leaders need to be arduous and do whatever it takes to maintain decorum and respect while in the field – at all times. It's a shame, really, because you would think someone interested in ghost hunting would know better. You'd expect them to be able to execute some common sense – maybe show a little empathy as well, but many of us have heard about how terrible it was to have paranormal teams on the premises.

Of course, there is the opposite side of that coin. Serious, responsible, well-behaved, pleasant and polite teams are also all over the place – taking care of business and trying to find answers. These groups need to represent the field, not the bad actors, because as with everything in life, it takes longer to build something than it does to tear it down.

But what does any of this have to do with EVP, right? I am certainly not the conscience of paranormal investigation by any means, and no one in charge of such things really cares what I have to say about it anyway. If I have any credibility it comes from EVP, and that's where the majority of my paranormal interests lie. Unfortunately, awful behavior reflects on everyone in the field, and I stand to lose a great many opportunities to learn because of the actions of these imbeciles. And, as much as I hate to say it, I really and truly believe that the spirits are watching us as well, and they don't dig it either.

To me, EVP currently represent our most productive technique of accumulating paranormal evidence, so results are important. EVP could be the thing that helps a troubled homeowner to make up her mind whether to stay or sell. A single EVP could be responsible for keeping someone up at night, so it better be for real and not some stupid team member horsing around in another part of the house. EVP come from way far away, and they are miraculous windows into a part of our existence that, as of yet, we cannot explain. But in order for an EVP to be presented as evidence, it has to endure a great deal of examination. The conditions for recording have got to be controlled and strictly adhered to.

Look. I like to have fun as much as the next person, and

believe me, I do. But EVP are important to me, and so far, that's been my main contribution in the paranormal arena. I intend to do what I'm supposed to in the right way, with a focused attitude, and with as much attention to detail as is humanly possible. When I present an EVP to a client, I need to be 100 percent positive it's righteous.

And when it is... when you've recorded that voice you know is going to help someone feel better about their life... Get it? Their life! When you present them with that voice, you're changing their impressions forever. It's a heady thing, and it makes for some serious soul-searching and suggests the need for a constantly renewed attitude toward the work.

I don't regret anything about getting involved with these voices from forever. They serve as proof that there is an afterlife and that the souls of our loved ones are ceaselessly connected with us. By listening to as many voices as I have, I've come to understand that what we refer to as "the other side" is actually a thriving, dynamic existence that seems to successfully hold the best and the worst of what was and is humanity. Hearing them speak has strengthened my religious beliefs and reinforced so many things I've been taught over the years. It makes me understand the value of faith as it offers just a small hint of the truth behind that faith.

So you have to "come correct" to the issue of EVP – respect is called for, without a doubt, and progressing the field may just hinge on what we continue to learn from our voices. As I see it, EVP represents our foothold into the paranormal, and they offer a stunning entry into that which has both plagued and edified mankind since the very beginning. Truly, once we have scrupulously labored over the authenticity of each EVP we record, what we are left with shines like gold nuggets on a beach, and they resonate like our grandfather's words always used to. Just as children learn when they listen, so do we learn from hearing. I am a listener. And what I hear is the generations of man somehow reaching out to let us know it's all good.

My father was a good and decent person who suffered more than his share of setbacks in life. Roadblocks, if you will – detours along the path less traveled. He didn't complain very much, and there was never any blame placed for his lot in life – he just dealt with it as it came, and never gave up, He fought his way through rare diseases and freak accidents, and he handled the eventual onset of both becoming deaf and blind at the same time, with great dignity and aplomb. He was a man's man and an athlete, a hard worker, and a friend to all. And if you spent any time with the man, you came away liking him, appreciating his sense of humor, and respecting his well-balanced sense of morality – never preachy, but always selfless and kind. He was a family man first, and I guess his children benefited the most from that; we always had him near. I always considered him wise, because he exhibited good judgment and such great common sense.

And I can talk about him all night and into the day;

stories about his youth, his college days, about how he won my mother... about his choices in life and why he made them. My father was a great man, and I was too small a man to recognize that until it was too late.

And I may never be able to identify his spirit; will never be able to say for sure that he is still around. That's okay – it is what it is. For all I know, there truly is just a heaven and a hell, and the voices I wish belonged to him are nothing more than passersby on their journey through purgatory.

But he was the kind of man worth looking for, and so he is worth that effort now. Wherever he is, and regardless of my success at finding him, even if I fail over and over, he is worth this journey. I have no choice but to make it – until there is either an end or an answer.

What started for me just 2 short years ago, will teach me so much and lead me in many directions, but I hesitate to recommend this road to everyone. Even though it has been good for me, I have a feeling not everyone is suited for it. Sometimes you can hear things you don't like or understand, and sometimes you feel creeped out in the worst way – not from fear, but from reality, and you have to be able to understand that the voices are, after all, just voices. Most of the time, you gain a sense of perspective and you better see your place in the scheme of things; gain an understanding of what you're made of; stare into an abyss you're not really sure is there. It's difficult to put into words, but sometimes the voices seem to be leading you down a dark passageway with no end in sight, unable to tell you that passageway is your life. They never try to live it for you, never try to steer you in any one direction – it's as if they are forbidden to do so, but it seems that they want you to recognize where you are and to understand where you should be. Just as they might do were they living.

And perhaps I'm making too much of it, but of course, I don't think so. I think a symbiotic relationship with the voices helps us to get along well and provides the comfort they need to be heard. And I know there are dreadful energies wherever they come from – the literature is already jam-packed with both truth and the fiction of that, but I know the good far outweighs the bad. There is little to fear, and much to be learned.

When I was a small boy, we lived near some woods, and I spent many summer days lying by the side of Stoney Run. I exhausted many a day looking up at the clouds, listening to the incredible sound of things, being amazed at the majestic scope of that place and the immense diversity of it all. It was a good place to learn lessons on your own. Sometimes a friend and I would walk through the water and get as wet as we could; look for crayfish and tadpoles, collect odd-shaped rocks, send our plans for the future off on the warm summer breezes.

Yeah, there was imagination on those breezes, and I could sometimes hear my name being called. I was reminded just how far away from home I was, and how near to day's end. Even though hearing my name called was quickly lost on the wind, and the ambient sounds that mix with thought and awareness, I could hear it clear enough. It was my mother's voice – it had to be – who else would it be? The sound of her distant voice would reach inside of me, and while I always knew it wasn't really there, it made me conscious once again. Time to go home. Her voice was so haunting and elusive, and of course, I did not answer, but I so wanted to believe, and secretly wished it were real. I'm told all children hear their mother's voice like that. It reminds them to be careful, and that they're loved; that it's time to come home.

But now, I wonder. They say you can't hear unless you listen, so maybe I've never stopped listening, but sometimes, what you perceive to be real is not. And sometimes it is. I think voices are meant to be heard – why else would someone speak, but to be heard? My first EVP said "Randy, ya gotta change." I think I have.

www.ingramcontent.com/pod-product-compliance
Lightning Source LLC
Chambersburg PA
CBHW071703090426

42738CB00009B/1647